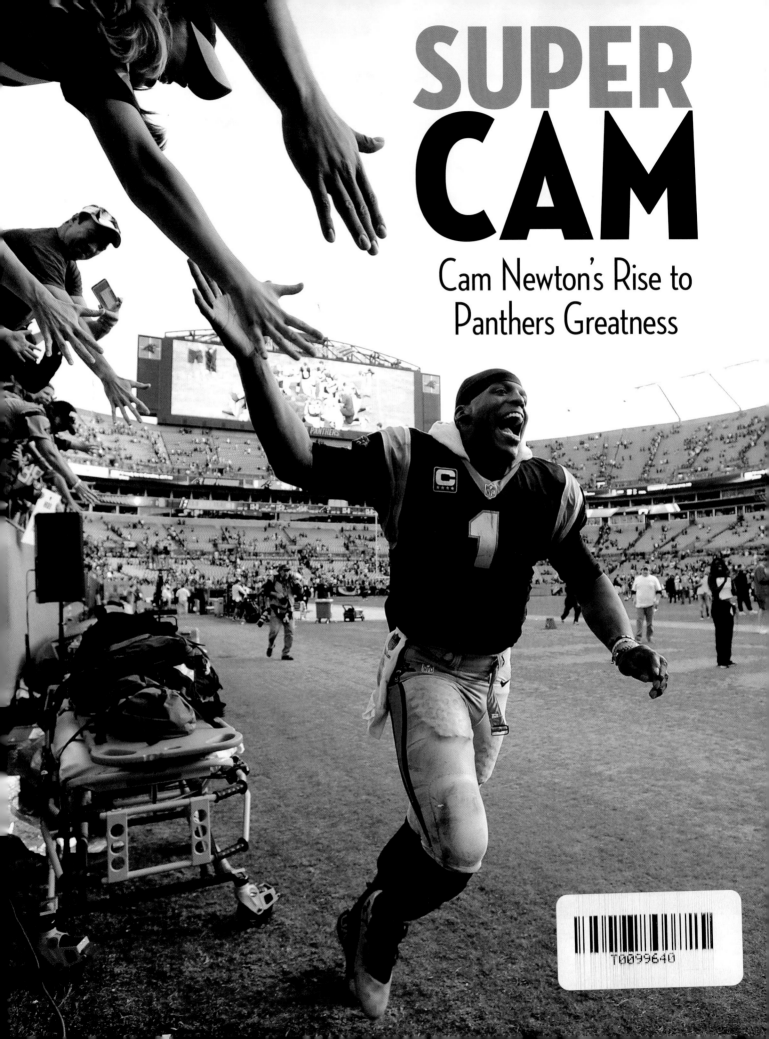

SUPER CAM

Cam Newton's Rise to Panthers Greatness

Cam Newton works his way down a line of fans seeking autographs during Newton's first training camp with the Panthers in August 2011. (Observer Photo/ David T. Foster III)

This book is available in quantity at special discounts for your group or organization.

For further information, contact:

Triumph Books LLC
814 North Franklin Street
Chicago, Illinois 60610
Phone: (312) 337-0747
www.triumphbooks.com

Printed in U.S.A.
ISBN: 978-1-62937-346-1

The Charlotte Observer
Publisher: Ann Caulkins
Editor: Rick Thames
Writers: Scott Fowler, Jonathan Jones, Joseph Person
Book editors: Gary Schwab, Mike Persinger, John Simmons (photo)
Photographers: David T. Foster III, Jeff Siner
Research: Maria David
Stories are from The Charlotte Observer and charlotteobserver.com

Design by Patricia Frey

Front and back cover photos by David T. Foster III

Contents

Shining Bright – On and Off the Field

Cam Dances, Celebrates His Way to Becoming MVP, International Star

By Jonathan Jones

Here's how big Cam Newton has become:

In her final year as first lady of the United States, Michelle Obama has enlisted Newton to help her Partnership for a Healthier America, a drive to help kids make healthier choices.

The smile, the dance, the celebrations... Newton is internationally known, and football sometimes almost seems inconsequential.

Charlotte has never seen an active player's star shine as brightly as Newton.

His impact came before he chose to wear No. 1 for the Carolina Panthers — a decision he made when his college number, 2, was already taken by Panthers quarterback Jimmy Clausen, and one he stayed with in 2012 when the number became available.

During his Heisman run at Auburn, Newton made famous the Superman pose that is now synonymous with him. Newton puts both hands to his chest and acts as if he's ripping open his button-up shirt to reveal the 'S' underneath.

Five years into the league, Newton continues to do it for each rushing touchdown — all 45 in the regular season and playoffs. And players at all levels imitate him.

Opponents mock Newton with the Superman pose after getting a sack or forcing a fumble against Newton. High school and college players have been doing it for years in admiration of Newton.

Cam Newton hands out hugs and high fives as he is swarmed by students on April 24, 2015. Approximately 800 students from more than 40 middle schools and academies attended Newton's School Pride Day at Memorial Stadium. (Observer Photo/John D. Simmons)

But Newton needed some help early on in developing the celebration.

"He was talking about it and doing it with one hand," Chad Froechtenicht, Newton's teammate at Blinn Junior College, said in an interview in 2015. "I said, 'Cam, Superman does it with two hands. You've got to rip it off. You've got to use two hands.' I corrected him, and then it just started from there."

Over the years, Newton has developed quite the cadre of sponsors. His time at Auburn, an Under Armour school, made his deal with the apparel giant an obvious one. Newton has also picked up deals with Gatorade, Beats by Dre, GMC, Dannon and Belk, with which he has his own clothing line.

Unique isn't a strong enough word to describe Newton's fashion style. When his MADE line launched in 2013, Newton seemed to dress more traditionally.

Over time that style morphed into more high-fashion — the kind of look you see on New York runways.

The man-pris pants, loafers with spikes, big Arby's-looking hats, foxtails attached to his belt loop. Newton is one-of-one when it comes to fashion.

His Nickelodeon show, "All in with Cam Newton," debuted in the summer of 2016. The 30-episode series matched kids with a mentor who helped the children follow their dreams. Newton's empire is expanding to children's television programming, where he's an executive producer.

Newton's play on the field is as good as it's ever been as evidenced by his NFL MVP

Cam Newton engages Berewick Elementary student Naomi Esperanza, 10, in getting the audience to cheer during Cam's Thanksgiving Jam in November 2013. Newton, along with members of his family and volunteers from Second Harvest Food Bank and The Fillmore, hosted the event. More than 800 kids and parents came out to be served a traditional Thanksgiving meal. (Observer Photo/T. Ortega Gaines)

Cam Newton bumps elbows with volunteers at Second Harvest Food Bank after helping to stuff boxes of food in December 2011. (Observer Photo/Diedra Laird)

award. He received 48 of a possible 50 votes for the league's ultimate individual title.

The blend of his 6-foot-5, 265-pound frame with his speed, physicality, arm strength and smarts is something rarely seen. It had been more than 20 years since a dual-threat quarterback won the league's MVP award (Steve Young, in 1994) before Newton took it home.

His rise in popularity is reflected in what fans are consuming.

From March 2013 until March 2014, Newton's NFL officially licensed merchandise — which includes jerseys, shirts and toys — ranked him as the 27th highest-selling player in the league. The following year he moved to 24th.

In 2015, he ranked seventh.

Newton's dancing has become one of the most popular, and divisive, aspects of today's NFL.

It's more than the Superman pose, the 1,000 megawatt smile or his traditional handing the touchdown football to little kids. Newton breaks out the latest dance craze — commonly from the hip-hop community — and incorporates that into his celebrations.

The one that caught on was the dab.

The beauty and genius behind the dab is that it's so easy to replicate. Someone with little to no rhythm can tuck their head into their arm and make a presentable dab.

Newton began doing it after rushing for first downs early in the 2015 season, but it didn't become a phenomenon until, after a game in Nashville against the Tennessee Titans, a Tennessee mom couldn't figure out what to tell her daughter about Newton's dancing.

The dab, which Newton adopted from the rap trio Migos, spread quickly.

European soccer players were doing it. Hockey players were, too. Young boys in the stands at basketball games would dab when the in-house camera put them on the video board.

Coaches and teammates say it's just Cam being Cam.

"You're looking at a man who's not afraid to be himself," comedian Kevin Hart said in 2015, when he and Ice Cube were with Newton in Charlotte promoting a film.

"I think what's great about Cam is that personality is what the sport needs. That flair. That spark. That ultimate level of swagger. I think so many people try to create personas and create characteristic traits that they think the world wants to see. Ultimately the world just wants to see you be you.

"And regardless of your color, race, shape or size, you can fit in as long as you're yourself because people know what they're getting into. People know what they're getting with this guy and he's having fun doing it. I'm loving watching it."

So is Charlotte. ✪

Cam Newton and his guests pose by growling during Newton's Christmas with Cam program on December 22, 2013. The Panthers' quarterback hosted 13 patients from Levine Children's Hospital. The participants watched the Panthers' game in a suite and were visited by Santa, Sir Purr and the TopCats. (Observer Photo/Jeff Siner)

Panthers Pin Hopes on Cam Newton

QB Says His Top Priority 'Is to Get with This Organization and Get Going.'

By Scott Fowler | April 29, 2011

The Carolina Panthers bet the house on Cam Newton, making him the No.1 overall pick in the NFL draft. The Panthers took possibly the biggest risk in franchise history by drafting Newton, hoping that he will lead them to big rewards as he did for Auburn in college. In one spectacular season, the quarterback won both a national championship and the Heisman Trophy while accounting for 50 total touchdowns.

The Panthers made their No.1 selection immediately Thursday night, within 10 seconds of the announcement that they were on the 10-minute "clock" teams get to make first-round picks. Newton quickly pulled on a Panthers hat that clashed with his pink tie, gave high-fives to his family and walked onstage to hold up a No.1 Panthers jersey alongside NFL commissioner Roger Goodell.

The loudspeakers blared "Cat Scratch Fever" as Newton gazed around Radio City Music Hall, soaking it all in with a dazzling smile that will become very familiar to Panthers fans. His father and his two brothers quickly put on Panthers' hats, too. Newton said later in a post-draft interview he only knew for sure he was the Panthers' pick when he heard his name called.

"My No.1 priority is to get with this organization and get going," Newton said. "I am moving to Charlotte ASAP."

When asked if he was ready to be the face of the Panthers' franchise, Newton said: "Absolutely. Absolutely. I'm ready to be in Charlotte and ready to get to work and take care of business."

What does Carolina now have with Newton? A quarterback who, at 6-foot-5 and 250 pounds, is larger than many linebackers. A magnetic personality who — when he wants to turn it on — can light up a roomful of kids or adults. And a number of questions, including how well he can learn an offense much more complicated

Cam Newton holds up a Panthers jersey with NFL commissioner Roger Goodell after Newton was selected as the No. 1 overall pick in the 2011 NFL Draft in New York. (AP Images)

The day after being chosen No. 1 by the Panthers in the NFL Draft, Cam Newton smiles as he receives an autographed hat from Adam Smith, the team's No. 1 pick in the Make-A-Wish draft. (Observer Photo/Jeff Siner)

than what Auburn ran in 2010 and how focused he will be once he inevitably becomes a multimillionaire.

Newton said he will be fueled by his numerous critics and that he understood being chosen No. 1 would make him even more of a target. Said Newton: "I understand that everybody is not just going to stop and just say, 'That's Cam. He's the No. 1 pick. And we can leave him alone.' If anything, the floodgates have opened officially."

Like all elite athletes, Newton has an ego. You could hear it in his voice Thursday when he was asked about comparisons to quarterback Vince Young, who has had a spotty NFL career.

Countered Newton: "I'm my own man. I'm my own athlete. I shouldn't be compared to anybody because the attributes I bring to this game are something I haven't really worked out. That's what I work at, and what I work to be — my own category."

Burdened by the worst offense in the NFL last season, the Panthers went 2-14. But Newton isn't necessarily expected to start right away at Carolina, which may be reticent to throw another rookie quarterback directly into the fire and returns second-year starter Jimmy Clausen.

As Newton's father, Cecil Newton, told me this week in New York: "It's not just going to just be an immediate impact. You're not going to go straight into the Super Bowl and start winning."

The elder Newton, of course, expects his son to eventually succeed. And many others do as well — assuming Newton stays out of the off-field trouble that occasionally dogged his collegiate career.

Eddie George, the former star NFL running back and now a broadcaster, told me Thursday before the draft: "Cam is a beast. He's got that Magic Johnson smile, and his athleticism speaks for itself. But now the biggest test comes, because everybody is going to want to ride his coattails, to be in his entourage. How will he handle that? Is he studying film, or is he out in the clubs? Because if he focuses on his craft and hones his skills, he could one day be the best quarterback in the NFL."

When the NFL introduced 25 top draft prospects to the crowd at Radio City Music Hall 30 minutes before the draft began, Newton drew both the most cheers and the most boos. It reminded me of NASCAR driver introductions back when the late Dale Earnhardt's name would get called.

Only Goodell drew more boos at this NFL draft than Newton (and the commissioner didn't receive any cheers, either), due to the current labor dispute between the NFL and its players. The rowdy crowd struck up a chant of "We want football!!"

"Me, too," Goodell said.

The Panthers' coaches want it, too, of course, because they need to get Newton started. And although the NFL labor dispute is still evolving, players have been cleared to resume working out at their club's facilities. Newton said he plans to fly to Charlotte, get a playbook and start studying it immediately.

"I'm ready to get this show on the road," Newton said. "And it warms my heart to go to an excellent city like Charlotte." ✪

Sweet in Defeat

Newton Is Spectacular in His Panthers Debut, Tying an NFL Record for the Most Passing Yards by a Rookie QB

By Joseph Person | September 12, 2011

Cam Newton began his pro career by lighting up the same field where his electric college career ended. And just like the BCS title game in January, Newton flung the ball all over University of Phoenix Stadium and led his offense up and down the field.

While confetti fell on Newton after Auburn beat Oregon for the national championship, there would be no storybook ending for the Panthers' quarterback Sunday.

He'll have to settle for one of the best passing performances by a rookie in NFL history.

Brushing off criticism that he could not succeed as a pro passer, Newton shredded the Arizona secondary for 422 yards and accounted for all three of the Panthers' touchdowns. But the Cardinals took advantage of secondary and special teams breakdowns by the Panthers to claim a 28-21 victory and spoil the debut of the No. 1 draft pick.

Newton broke the record held by Peyton Manning (302) for passing yards by a rookie in Week 1 and equaled Matthew Stafford's record yardage total for rookies. Stafford, the No. 1 overall pick of Detroit, threw for 422 yards against Cleveland in Week 10 in 2009.

Since 1960, only three quarterbacks have passed for more yards in a season opener than Newton: Dan Marino (473 in 1994), Kurt Warner (441 in 2000) and Manning (433 in 2010).

"That's some rare company to beat out. And then your first crack out of the box," Panthers left tackle Jordan Gross said. "He's only going to get better from here. He didn't even really scramble and do anything with his legs. I'm excited to be on a team with him. Our offense is much improved and I expect us to get a lot better next week."

Cam Newton throws downfield during the Panthers' loss to the Arizona Cardinals on September 11, 2011. Newton became the first rookie to throw for more than 400 yards in his NFL debut. (Observer Photo/David T. Foster III)

Newton completed 24 of 37 passes and finished with a passer rating of 110.4. He had two touchdowns — both to Steve Smith, covering 77 and 26 yards — and one interception.

But he couldn't get the Panthers into the end zone on five tries from the 11 or closer in the final two minutes, and was not in the mood for celebrating afterward.

"Cam's very disappointed," said Smith, who had eight catches for 178 yards. "I'm encouraged by that."

Despite Smith's big day, he was not targeted with the game on the line. Panthers coach Ron Rivera, who also was making his debut, said Smith was the first read on at least one of the plays.

Said Smith: "Some I was and some I was there to occupy the safety. That's my job in certain situations, and I tried to do it to the best of my abilities."

On first down from the 11, Newton threw a ball that bounced off tailback Mike Goodson's hands. After Newton twice overthrew Legedu Naanee, tight end Greg Olsen came down with Newton's fourth-down pass out of bounds.

But the Cardinals were offside on the play. On fourth-and-5 from the 6 with 1 minute, 19 seconds left, Newton threw a short pass to Goodson, who was stopped by linebacker Paris Lenon a yard short of the

Cam Newton gives a jump and bump greeting to Eric Norwood before the Panthers' 2011 season opener against the Arizona Cardinals. (Observer Photo/David T. Foster III)

first down. Though Olsen was open on the play, Goodson was the first option out of the backfield.

"We felt our matchup was better than theirs. We could have gotten in," Newton said. "We missed some opportunities. That game didn't come down to the last play."

The Panthers led 21-14 entering the final quarter after Newton's first touchdown run — a 1-yard dive that capped an 80-yard drive.

But the Cardinals caught Carolina in a blitz on their first possession of the fourth quarter. With the Panthers sending their linebackers, Kevin Kolb threw short to Early Doucet, who ran through a poor tackle attempt by safety Jordan Pugh and went 70 yards to make it 21-all.

Pugh said he blew his assignment on the play. He was supposed to be in man coverage on Doucet, but got crossed up and was nowhere near Doucet when he caught Kolb's pass.

"I take all the blame on that," Pugh said. "That's all on me."

When the Panthers' next drive stalled at the Arizona 47, punter Jason Baker came out for a rugby-type kick designed to pin the Cardinals deep. But rookie Patrick Peterson, the fifth pick in the April draft, fielded it at the 11, found a crease and went 89 yards for the go-ahead score with 7:15 left.

The Panthers' outside gunners, including Pugh, were behind Peterson when he caught it after running past him to get in position to down the punt.

"It's one of those gray areas for us as gunners," Pugh said. "You try to play both,

and it backfired. But he made a heck of a play, too."

Peterson almost was burned by a little showboating. He slowed around the 15-yard line, but sped up when he saw Goodson closing on him.

"I was gonna give you guys a taste of my dancing skills," Peterson said. "I couldn't. I took a quick peek and I saw him behind me and was like, 'Oh, I gotta get there now,' and that's when I dove in for the touchdown."

The big plays were the difference in a game when the Panthers outgained Arizona 422 to 309 in passing yardage, had 11 more first downs and held more than a five-minute edge in time of possession.

"We had a couple of momentum swings that really took the wind out of our sail, offensively and defensively," Rivera said. "But the bottom line is we can't have that. We're too young a football team to survive self-inflicted wounds. And we have nobody to blame but ourselves."

Newton's record-setting day gives hope to a team that had little of it during a 2-14 finish in 2010.

"There's been a lot of good rookies that have played this game. And to be No. 1, that's a pretty special mark — on the road, in that kind of environment," Olsen said.

"It's a true testament to the type of player he is, and athlete he is. He's just one of those guys when he gets in the game, there's just something about him. There's some guys that have it, and some don't."

Under the retractable roof in the stadium he owns, Newton had it Sunday. ✪

Cam Newton makes the Superman gesture after rushing for a touchdown in his NFL debut against the Arizona Cardinals. (AP Images)

The Best NFL Rookie Season Ever?

Newton's Record-Setting Debut Season Puts QB in Rare Company

By Scott Fowler | January 14, 2012

Let's get this out of the way first: There is no award called "Best NFL Rookie Season Ever." There is no vote. It's purely a mythical title.

It's also a great debate. The Carolina Panthers' Cam Newton has become a contender for the title because of a 2011 season in which he became the first rookie quarterback to throw for more than 4,000 yards and the first quarterback ever to rush for 14 touchdowns.

Newton accounted for a rookie-record 35 touchdowns overall — he had 21 passing touchdowns. And when the 6-5, 244-pound Newton begins running and gets beyond the defensive linemen and into a defense's secondary, he's frequently bigger than the players trying to bring him down.

"There are guys out there in the back half of NFL defenses making business decisions

at that point," said Herm Edwards, a former NFL player and coach for 30 years who is now an ESPN analyst. "They're going, 'I don't really want to tackle this guy.' Cam is a whole different sort of cat. His athleticism is just like, 'Really?! Really?!'"

But were 35 total touchdowns for a 6-10 team enough to grab the title of "Best Rookie Season Ever"? Peter King of *Sports Illustrated* believes so. But do you? Would you consider Newton's rookie season better than:

- Lawrence Taylor, who started redefining the position of outside linebacker as a rookie out of North Carolina in 1981 and ended up being named AP Defensive Player of the Year? Not just rookie of the year, mind you — best defensive player in the league.

Cam Newton tries to avoid going out of bounds as Detroit's Cliff Avril pursues him during the Panthers' 49-35 win over the Lions on November 20, 2011. (Observer Photo/David T. Foster III)

- Eric Dickerson, who led the entire league in rushing with 1,808 yards in 1983 and scored 18 rushing touchdowns?
- Dick "Night Train" Lane, who set an NFL record as a rookie in 1952 with 14 interceptions that still stands 60 years later — in a 12-game season?
- Randy Moss, who in 1998 led the NFL with 17 receiving TDs as a rookie and had 1,313 receiving yards?
- Ben Roethlisberger, who in 2004 went 14-1 as a rookie starting quarterback, including 13-0 in the regular season?

There are many more contenders. You might be surprised for instance, that roughly half of the AP Offensive Rookies of the Year have been running backs. There have been more than 50 cases of an NFL rookie running back rushing for more than 1,000 yards (with Dickerson's total still the rookie high-water mark). In statistical terms, it's not uncommon at all.

Cam Newton fends off Detroit's Nick Fairley during the Panthers' November 2011 win over the Lions. (Observer Photo/David T. Foster III)

Above: Newton laughs during Carolina's December 2011 win at Tampa Bay. (Observer Photo/Jeff Siner)

'RIGHT INTO THE FIRE'

There have been fewer great rookie years by NFL quarterbacks, in large part because even the best of the bunch often sat behind a veteran in their first season. Dan Marino played barely more than half a season as a rookie — throwing 20 touchdown passes and only six interceptions and starting in the Pro Bowl. Peyton Manning started in 1998 and had 26 TDs — still the rookie record — but he also threw 28 interceptions and went 3-13 for Indianapolis.

NFL teams more frequently start rookie quarterbacks for an entire season these days. Joe Flacco, Mark Sanchez and Roethlisberger have all experienced success as rookies in the past decade. All three had the benefit of strong defenses and were more "game-manager" types of quarterbacks in their first year, asked more often not to lose a game than to win it. Roethlisberger, for instance, averaged about one touchdown pass and less than 200 passing yards per game his rookie season.

Of the seven rookies to throw for more than 3,000 yards with at least 10 touchdown passes, four of them came in the past four years (Matt Ryan, Sam Bradford, Newton and Andy Dalton). In Cincinnati, Dalton got the Bengals to the playoffs this season and is Newton's main competitor for the offensive rookie-of-the-year honors.

Newton dwarfed Dalton in rushing touchdowns (14 to one). The two were very close in touchdown passes (21 for Newton, 20 for Dalton). Newton had more interceptions (17 to 13).

"The one area I'd say was problematic for Newton and different from, say, Andy Dalton, was the turnovers," said Eric Mangini, who has been the head coach for two NFL teams and now works for ESPN. "That's the only thing that weighs down the season. As explosive as he was offensively, that would be the one area where I would have concern."

Tim Hasselbeck, an NFL quarterback for six years who now works as an ESPN analyst, had a more positive view.

"Factor in that Cam was thrown right into the fire, not having time to get many reps because of the lockout before training camp," Hasselbeck said. "When you look at it from that perspective, what he did this season is without a doubt as impressive as any rookie quarterback I've ever seen."

King, the *Sports Illustrated* writer, wrote one sentence in the Jan. 9 *SI* issue saying he believed Newton's rookie season was the best ever and then magnified his point at my request.

"He broke the rookie record for passing yards in a season," King wrote in an email to me about Newton. "He broke the record for rushing touchdowns by a quarterback — and he's a third of the way to breaking the career record for rushing touchdowns by a quarterback. He accounted for more touchdowns than any rookie ever. The Panthers scored 210 more points this year than last. Is it a coincidence that Newton accounted for 210 points? He did — 35 touchdowns, times six. That's 210."

THE IMPACT OF "LT"

There are dozens of numbers you can analyze from Newton's season. What Taylor did in 1981, though, was harder to quantify. Sacks weren't even an official NFL statistic at the time, although he had 9.5 of them unofficially. But until Taylor, outside linebackers looked different.

"They were good about playing the run, but they were sort of heavy-legged," said Edwards, who was a cornerback in the NFL then. "Then Taylor came and his athleticism was off the charts. He changed the way linebackers were viewed."

NFL teams in those days often lined up in the "I" formation, with the fullback directly behind the quarterback and the tailback behind him, about eight yards deep. The offense would then run a sweep to one side and leave unblocked the outside linebacker on the other side, figuring the tailback could outrun that player anyway. Taylor chased down the tailback so frequently from behind that many NFL teams either stopped using the "I" formation entirely against the Giants or

Cam Newton tries to get rid of the ball to avoid being sacked by Detroit's Kyle Vanden Bosch in November 2011. (Observer Photo/David T. Foster III)

at least blocked it differently. Teams began looking for faster linebackers in Taylor's mold.

Quarterbacks win the various rookie-of-the-year awards far less frequently than running backs or linebackers. Quarterback is the most complex position in football, one in which eye-popping athleticism isn't enough. JaMarcus Russell was the overall No. 1 pick in the NFL draft in 2007 precisely because he could throw a football 70 yards with some accuracy. But Russell isn't even in the league anymore because he wasn't able to handle everything else that went along with the position.

Running backs often make a bigger impact more quickly. There have been 16 rookie running backs to rush for more than 1,300 yards (only three rookie wide receivers have reached that number). Those running backs range from hall of famers like Dickerson and Barry Sanders (1,470) to those with solid but ultimately unspectacular NFL careers like Rueben Mayes (1,353) and South Carolina's George Rogers (1,674).

But what about game-changers like Taylor — players who turned a position on its head and made everyone look at it in a new way?

There have been only a few. In 1965, the graceful Gale Sayers entered the league with a flourish and put a premium on speed. His yardage numbers weren't

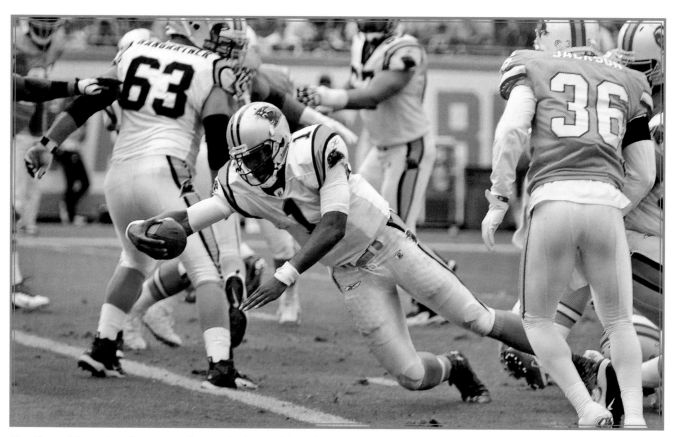

Cam Newton falls into the end zone to score his second rushing touchdown of the game against Tampa Bay on December 4, 2011. Newton set the NFL single-season record for rushing touchdowns by a quarterback in 2011. (Observer Photo/Jeff Siner)

incredible, but his 22 touchdowns included 14 rushing, six receiving and two on returns.

In 1998, Randy Moss came out of Marshall and did much the same thing. He had dropped to No. 21 in the first round because of character concerns (the Panthers chose defensive end Jason Peter at No. 14 instead of Moss).

Moss then became a game-changer, with a combination of size (6-4, 210) and speed that more than compensated for his rawness. "What he did as a rookie was just phenomenal," Edwards said. "He lined up on the left side and never moved. When they crossed the 50, he was always running vertical (to the end zone). And you couldn't stop him."

Moss' 17 receiving touchdowns led the NFL that season as the Vikings went 15-1 (but lost in the playoffs).

MY FINAL RANKING

I would argue that Newton is another game-changer. Certainly there have been mobile quarterbacks before him who could throw — Randall Cunningham, Michael Vick and so on. But Newton, as Edwards said, is truly a "whole different sort of cat." His accuracy, his ability to think on the field and his work ethic were all underrated coming out of college. And he is the best athlete on a football field every time he steps on it.

Also, remember this: Jimmy Clausen had almost the same offensive cast as Newton in 2010, and the Panthers' offense was the worst in the NFL. Newton's win-loss record will get better in conjunction with the Panthers' defense, but he's already

amazing. He was the first quarterback ever to throw for 4,000 yards and rush for at least 500 yards in the same season.

As I've written before, I believe Newton's maturity level needs some work. He can be more of a leader. He can work on his sideline body language and his occasional interview misstep. I think that will come. Newton is, after all, only 22.

When I asked Edwards, Hasselbeck and Mangini point-blank if Newton's rookie season was the best ever, none of them wanted to go there. They all deflected the question.

Noted Edwards: "After 30 years of playing and coaching in the league, I only have a couple of definites. One is that the best player in the NFL, ever, was Jim Brown. And I can tell you for sure the best cornerback ever was Deion Sanders. Other than that, I sort of leave all the absolutes alone."

That's fine. But ultimately, I'm with King. After analyzing the numbers, I would rank the top five rookie seasons this way, in order:

1. Cam Newton, Panthers, 2011.
2. Lawrence Taylor, N.Y. Giants, 1981.
3. Randy Moss, Minnesota, 1998.
4. Dick "Night Train" Lane, L.A. Rams, 1952.
5. Eric Dickerson, L.A. Rams, 1983.

You don't agree? More power to you. But to me, Newton's rookie season was so remarkable that it deserves to be ranked No. 1. The big question now is this:

What's he going to do for an encore? ✪

CAM
MOMENT

MR. MOPEYHEAD

Cecil Newton has seen it after backyard basketball battles, high school football games — even after a coed church softball game.

The head down, forlorn face, sagging shoulders look — everything except maybe the white Gatorade towel that has become as much a part of Panthers quarterback Cam Newton's NFL persona as his head-turning touchdown runs and his signature Superman celebration.

The rest of the world might be weighing in on it now, but Newton's parents have seen their son struggle with losses and get frustrated when his performance wasn't perfect since the first time the grade-schooler strapped on his shoulder pads for the North Clayton Eagles in suburban Atlanta.

But Cecil and Jackie Newton view Newton's downcast demeanor after losses much like Panthers coach Ron Rivera does — a sign of Newton's intense competitive drive, and only a conversation topic if the Panthers aren't winning.

Newton's competitiveness has led to championships at every level, from the three-year unbeaten streak his Pop Warner team had while Newton was on the squad to the two national titles he won at Blinn Junior College and Auburn.

Newton is not accustomed to losing. When he does, he's not given to putting on a happy face in front of his teammates or the media. Rivera jokingly referred to him as "Mr. Mopeyhead" during his rookie season.

The issue took off after receiver Steve Smith "lit into" Newton for sitting on the bench rather than standing with his teammates near the end of a 36-7 loss to the Giants in a Sept. 20, 2012, game.

"If we weren't the only game on and we win the game it's not an issue. Let's be honest about that first and foremost," Rivera said. "The young man knows he has to continue to work on himself."

—Joseph Person

The Evolution of Cam Newton

Quarterback Working on Leadership, with an Assist from Ex-Panther Jake Delhomme

By Jonathan Jones | September 7, 2013

It's a blend of nerves and restlessness that keeps Cam Newton awake nights before NFL games.

He scrolls through his iTunes account, buying music and assembling new playlists. He watches "SportsCenter," replaying the day's college football highlights so often that he knows what the anchors will say before they say it.

"I'm good if I go to sleep by 1," Newton said. "I've been up til 4 o'clock. Look at the clock and it's 1:30. Look back at the clock, it's 3:15. What?"

It's Year 3 for Cam Newton as quarterback of the Carolina Panthers. Most often seen in public with his magnetic smile and Superman-pose confidence, he's coming off a year in which he and the Panthers finished strong but missed the playoffs. He broke even more records but was routinely criticized for his demeanor and interactions with teammates.

"I think there's a misunderstanding with me," Newton said in a recent 90-minute interview with the *Observer*. "Yeah, I like to look good. Yeah, I like to have fun. Yeah, I have a passion and I'm goofy and I wear my emotions on my sleeve. Maybe I'm a sore loser or maybe I'm not the best person to lose a game with, but who is? When it comes down to this game, and if you're on my side, I'm with you."

He says he wants to be the best teammate and leader possible and this past offseason he looked hard at himself. He studied not only game film but also his post-game press conferences. He thinks he's misunderstood, but he also now has a better understanding of why and is making adjustments.

More than anything, Newton would like to put the Panthers into the playoffs — winning cures a lot, he says. He's even gotten advice from Jake Delhomme, a former Carolina quarterback who didn't

Cam Newton leaps onto Panthers cornerback Josh Norman's back after Norman intercepted a pass during a 2013 preseason game against the Pittsburgh Steelers. (Observer Photo/Jeff Siner)

have the physical skills Newton has, but who was adored by teammates and fans alike as he took the Panthers to the Super Bowl a decade ago.

Now, as another NFL season begins, when Newton can't sleep it's because he knows he has something to prove.

STARTING OVER IN TEXAS

In 2009, Newton was somewhere he never expected to be.

He had been highly recruited out of Atlanta's Westlake High and spent his first two years at Florida before an arrest for a laptop theft derailed his time in Gainesville in 2008.

He transferred from Florida, which won the BCS National Championship that year, to Blinn, a junior college in Brenham, Texas, with an enrollment of about 5,000 students. There, he says, he began to remake himself.

Gone were the days of unlimited Nike cleats, sweatbands, armbands and other extras that come with a top football program. At Blinn, you got one pair of cleats and socks. Some players, Newton said, resorted to stealing shoelaces from a nearby sporting goods store.

His teammates were shocked when he told them about all the gear he received at Florida. They'd ask him what his ex-teammates, including Heisman-winning quarterback Tim Tebow and star wide receiver Percy Harvin, were like. And often, Newton held court in the Texas junior college cafeteria.

"Many times I would be at a dining hall and it would start with two or three people and it would end with 13 or 20 people I'm talking to saying, 'Look man, you wouldn't believe this,'" Newton said.

He says he learned how to fit in with people who weren't like him. From suburban Atlanta, Newton was one of the few Blinn players who was not from Texas. He acclimated himself to the music, the style of dress and the Texas accents.

Blinn went 11-1, won the National Junior College Athletic Association National Championship and Newton eventually chose Auburn as his next destination. He remembers one particular day with his Blinn teammates, and the connection they had.

With a handful of teammates around him on the field, Newton, in full uniform in the middle of the crowd, began rapping for a nearby camera. Blinn players chimed in rhythmically with "Uh's" between pauses.

"On my car," Newton began a new verse.

"You ain't got no car!" a teammate deadpanned and Newton collapsed in laughter.

"It was so pure, man," Newton said recently, smiling. "I went there with nothing and I left with everything."

'THE WRONG ATTITUDE'

As a college junior, he led Auburn to an undefeated season, an SEC championship, a BCS national championship and won the Heisman Trophy before the Panthers took him No.1 overall in the 2011 NFL draft.

Newton was "unconscious" in his first NFL game, he says. He passed for 422 yards, shattering the previous rookie debut record by more than 100 yards, and accounted for three touchdowns.

Panthers wide receiver Steve Smith (left) shares a laugh with Cam Newton on the Panthers' bench during a 2013 preseason game. (Observer Photo/Jeff Siner)

But a late-fourth quarter fourth-down completion came up 2 yards short of the goal line and the Panthers lost to the Cardinals, 28-21.

Newton was inconsolable after the loss. Later, he would cry.

"I was so paralyzed," Newton remembers. "I didn't talk to nobody. It was awkward. I made the situation so awkward. I would come in that locker room and I wouldn't talk to nobody. Nobody. Nobody.

"I just felt like nobody understood or felt like I felt, which was absolutely the wrong attitude."

The losses mounted and Newton's demeanor hardly changed. It came to a head in Week 3 of the 2012 season when the Panthers lost 36-7 to the Giants at home on national television.

Veteran wide receiver Steve Smith lit into Newton for sulking on the bench while backup Derek Anderson played out

the fourth quarter. Newton's postgame news conference mirrored his sideline composure and he offered a suggestion box to anyone in the media who had an answer to the Panthers' woes.

Five weeks later, Newton was criticized for not congratulating wide receiver Louis Murphy when he recovered a Newton fumble in the end zone for a touchdown. Both players later said it wasn't an issue, and Murphy said he wasn't looking for thanks.

"You don't get a bubble or a ding to tell you the camera's on you," Newton said. "Sometimes you don't understand how much you impact something, or you may take it for granted. It was nothing ever against my teammates. It's just that I'm so — and I've got to tone it down to a degree — but my competitive nature will never be flushed out of my body."

Questions about Newton's demeanor now not only draws a sigh from the quarterback, but also from his teammates.

Running back DeAngelo Williams has grown tired of people questioning his teammate. The quarterback position is a leadership role whether one wants to be a leader or not, he says, and Newton has the qualities to be one.

"He's a leader, regardless of what the outside people say about Cam or how they see him in terms of his body language and things like that," Williams said when Newton was named a team captain. "Until you know the guy, you don't understand the body language. He hates losing a great deal, and it bothers him when he doesn't perform

well or to his standards. He holds himself to a higher standard than anybody can ever imagine.

"Nobody is under more scrutiny than Cam or any other quarterback that hasn't produced in terms of winning."

Smith said that when the losses began piling up, Newton, who has a 13-19 record in the NFL, could have flamed out like several other high-profile young quarterbacks.

Instead, Smith said Newton has navigated his way through the NFL to find what it means to be a franchise quarterback and a leader of 52 other men in the locker room.

"Being the first overall pick, coming in here and being viewed as the guy who's going to help save the organization, it's a lot of pressure," Smith said. "As we've seen in the past, a lot of other players have not handled themselves as well — Todd Marinovich, Jeff George, a lot of guys who weren't mentally capable of handling themselves or physically. I think he has the ability and the desire, not to just be a great player, but he also wants to be a great teammate.

"He's like every other young man that's in the working world. He's trying to find his way in a constructive, healthy way. Has he made some mistakes along the way? We all have."

GLIMPSE OF JAKE

Panthers coach Ron Rivera had Jake Delhomme address the team on Aug.21, a few hours before they took a flight to

Cam Newton walks off the field after throwing an interception during the second half of the Panthers' 22-6 loss to the Arizona Cardinals in 2013. (Observer Photo/David T. Foster III)

Baltimore for the third exhibition of the preseason.

A decade ago, Delhomme was the quarterback who led the Panthers to their only Super Bowl appearance — the city's greatest professional sports moment. He stayed in Charlotte through the 2009 season.

There are a handful of Delhomme's former teammates left, but most of the players in the meeting room in August had never heard the quarterback speak to the team.

Newton was amazed by Delhomme that day — what he said, and the conviction with which he said it.

Delhomme had something Newton coveted: Jake had the room.

"I've talked to him one-on-one a couple times, but I had never seen that side of him," Newton said. "From what I saw, he had everybody in that room just..."

Newton snaps his fingers.

"He just had them. Not saying that I don't got it, but he put it in a way that, you would have thought Jake Delhomme was a Hall of Fame quarterback the way he was talking. And that's what I want."

Delhomme said he just spoke from the heart. He was only supposed to talk five minutes, but that didn't happen.

He told the current Panthers how privileged they are to be playing in the NFL. That at 38 years old and with 15 years of NFL experience, he still yearns to get back to the field.

He misses the practice field, the games, playing in the NFL. But more importantly, he misses playing in Charlotte.

"I tried to explain to them that you've got to embrace your time here in Carolina with the Panthers because it's not that way in other places," Delhomme said. "There are some good places, don't get me wrong, but this is a special place.

"The beginning of each season is always something that, you never know what could happen. It could be great, it could be so-so and it could be terrible. When it's great in Carolina, man I'm telling you, it's really great."

Delhomme lives in his native Louisiana. He says he won't go to the Mercedes-Benz Superdome, home of the New Orleans Saints, unless the Panthers are playing.

CAM AND CAROLINA

Is Newton all in for Carolina?

According to the NFL's collective bargaining agreement, a player can begin re-negotiating his contract following his third season.

Newton signed a four-year, $22 million deal in 2011 that has a club option for a fifth year. He'll make more than that in his second contract, but it's a matter of how much and, more importantly for Carolina fans, when and where.

"Would I want to? Absolutely," Newton said, when asked if he wants to make a long-term commitment to Charlotte and the Panthers. "But what people don't understand is, there's still a business. Charlotte will always have a place in my heart. Who am I to say I will be in Charlotte for 15 years? Who am I to say this is my last year? I don't want to put that thought in anybody's mind, because if I do that, I'm cheating my teammates."

He'll worry about the contract details when it's time, he says. But so far, he's made his roots in Charlotte. Along with his national endorsement deals, Newton has partnered with Carolinas Healthcare Systems to promote healthy lifestyles for children. Newton's foundation put on School Pride Day for 40 area middle schools in the spring and funded a 7-on-7 tournament for local high school teams this summer.

"We all know that contracts come up and some go according to plan and some of them don't," Newton said. "Whether the team has money or not, whether the player wants to play for the team or not.

"I've said it numerous times where my heart is, and it's no secret. It's up to me to control what's going on right now."

Year 3 begins for Newton like the previous two: Pregnant with expectations but with a fan base bracing itself for another subpar season.

Newton says he wants to feel in Charlotte what he felt at Auburn. Newton said he wasn't just playing the game for himself, but for so many other people.

When he first came to Charlotte in 2011, Newton says he did a double-take when he saw Giants or Redskins flags on cars. In Auburn, fans schedule weddings around the Tigers' schedule and the school erects 10-foot bronze statues for Heisman winners.

Newton says he's starting to feel that excitement in Charlotte. He says he will take what he learned this offseason and apply it to his game and to leading the team.

That includes all he learned from Delhomme, from both hearing him command a room to their one-on-one conversations.

Here's what Delhomme told Newton:

"I've never been in Cam's situation — first overall pick, Heisman Trophy. I've never been under that type of microscope. I said if you need anything I'll be here. He knows how I feel about Charlotte and the Panthers, and I said, 'Hey, you could own this town and own this team,' and that's what I've told him the couple of times I've seen him.

"Do the right thing, Charlotte will embrace you, and it could be good for a long time." ✪

Cam Newton rubs his head on the bench during the Panthers' loss to the New Orleans Saints in December 2013. (Observer Photo/David T. Foster III)

The Young Receivers

Cam Newton Gives Kids Footballs and Lasting Memories

By Scott Fowler | December 28, 2013

One football at a time. That's how Cam Newton has created indelible memories for dozens of kids at Carolina Panthers games.

The Carolina quarterback started handing footballs to children in October 2011 after the Panthers scored a touchdown. Since then he has given away several dozen in what has become one of the most beloved traditions in team history.

But where did all those footballs go? Newton, for one, never had any idea how deep of an impression the footballs made upon the kids and families that received them.

For the past month, I have been working on reuniting some of the "Cam Football Kids" with the charismatic quarterback. That process culminated Monday, when Newton walked into a locker room at Bank of America Stadium filled with 15 of those rambunctious, happy children and charmed them all over again.

Well, all of them except one. But we'll get to that.

The children huddled around Newton, telling him stories about sleeping with their footballs and taking them to school. One girl — 12-year-old Hannah Garthright of Charlotte — also had written him a letter.

"You gave me a football and I wanted to say thank you," she wrote. "I have hearing aids and ADHD, and when I see the Panthers get a touchdown, it makes me think that I can do that too — only a little bit different, because I play basketball. You inspire me by letting me know that I can do anything. P.S. — I like your smile."

Newton had the kids laughing immediately when they told him about the footballs that sometimes shared their pillows.

"You know what a football is made of?" he asked. "That's an ol' dead pig right there. You're sleeping with a pig!"

Panthers fans anxiously wait for Cam Newton to deliver a touchdown football to the stands during a November 2015 home game. (Observer Photo/Jeff Siner)

But before we hear more from Newton and his holiday huddle with the kids, let's back up a little. How did this tradition begin?

'GIVE IT TO A LITTLE KID'

Newton made an enormous impact in 2011, his rookie year with the Panthers. He threw for more than 400 yards in each of his first two games and was such an effective runner that he would set an NFL record for quarterbacks with 14 rushing touchdowns.

He also came into the league with a ready-made, TV-friendly TD celebration. Newton would pretend he was Clark Kent turning into Superman and mime the gesture in which Kent rips off his dress shirt to reveal the "S" underneath.

But for the first six games of his NFL career, Newton didn't hand out touchdown balls. The tradition actually started at the suggestion of Mike Shula, then the Panthers' quarterbacks coach and now the offensive coordinator.

When Newton scored against Washington in a home game Oct. 23, 2011, he still had the ball he scored with in his hand as he began the "Superman" routine. Shula's voice, as usual, was being piped directly into Newton's helmet headset — that is a standard NFL routine to allow play calls to get to the quarterback more easily.

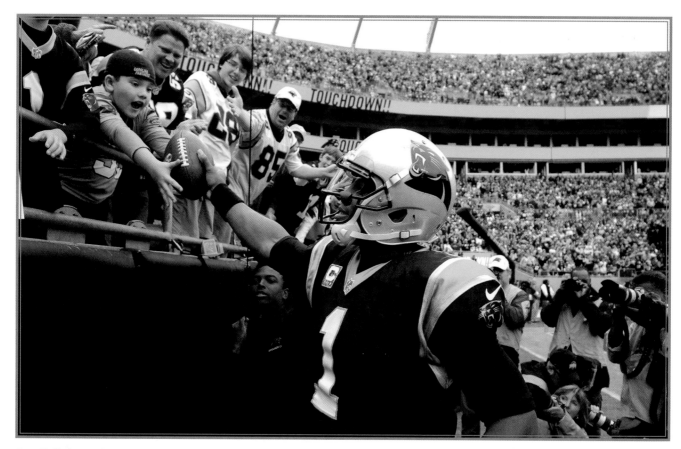

Grant Tadlock, an eight-year-old boy from Charlotte, receives a football from Cam Newton after the Panthers scored a second quarter touchdown during Carolina's win over the Green Bay Packers on November 8, 2015. (Observer Photo/Jeff Siner)

Recounted Newton shortly after the game: Shula "says when you celebrate, it's not a celebration unless you give back. He says, 'You do all that riffraff, whatever you do, but at the end you give that football to a little kid. You find a little kid.'

"So after I did whatever I did," Newton continued, "I heard somebody (Shula) in my headset saying, 'Give it to a little kid! Give it to a little kid!' I looked and there was this kid just gleaming from ear to ear, so I gave it to him."

Shula politely declined to be interviewed for this article. "That's all Cam," the coach said of the giveaways. "He has made that tradition his own."

The first handoff went to 10-year-old Law Waddill of Raleigh. His reaction in the immediate aftermath would turn out to be typical of many of the "Cam Football Kids."

"I was shaking and sweating," Law said. "There were tears in my eyes. It was really weird. Here was this Heisman Trophy winner, giving me a ball that he scored with."

Law and his 10-year-old cousin Nathan Guptill — who lives in Charlotte and was right behind Law when Newton handed up the ball — decided to share custody. They both came to the photo shoot Monday with Newton.

"So you were the first ones, huh?" Newton said, smiling at Law and Nathan.

'IF I HAD A WISH LIST'

Since Newton began the tradition, the Panthers have scored slightly more than 100 touchdowns. No one keeps count, but I would estimate Newton has given away the ball on close to half of those.

Grant Tadlock and his dad, Bryan Tadlock, cheer for the Panthers after Cam Newton handed Grant a football following a Panthers touchdown. (Observer Photo/Jeff Siner)

The way it works: Newton always gives it away when he scores himself (he started off only doing the giveaway on his own touchdowns). And now he often gives it away, too, when another Carolina offensive player scores.

When he's choosing a child, it takes about five seconds. He runs around, looks for big smiles and tries to spread the footballs into different corners of the stadium. Newton frequently picks a child in a Cam Newton jersey, but not always. The lucky kids usually turn out to be between ages 7 and 14.

Occasionally, other offensive players have chosen to either keep their own touchdown balls or give them away themselves, so not all home-game TD balls end up in the stands courtesy of the quarterback. Newton also doesn't give the

Ten-year-old Tatum Anderson of Columbia, Maryland, celebrates after receiving a football from Cam Newton during an October 2012 game against the Dallas Cowboys. (Observer Photo/Jeff Siner)

balls away on defensive touchdowns, so the "Sunday giveaway," as he and other Panthers call it, is hit or miss.

On road games, sometimes Newton finds a friendly kid in a Panthers jersey nearby — Hannah Garthright got hers in Miami this year on a mother-daughter trip to the Panthers-Dolphins game. Sometimes he doesn't.

The NFL doesn't fine Newton for giving footballs away, according to a league spokesman. But all NFL players are fined $5,250 when they throw or punt a ball into the stands because of issues of crowd safety. That's what Newton did on the winning touchdown in the New England game Nov. 18, when he excitedly threw the ball 16 rows into the stands, above where the T-shirt guns often reach. That was a $5,250 throw.

Normally, though, Newton tamps down his excitement enough to hand the ball to someone like Charlotte's Jack Schoening, 11.

Schoening was out of town and couldn't come to our photo shoot, but he got a ball from Newton on Oct. 20, 2013, four days before his birthday.

"If I had a wish list for things I wanted to accomplish in my life," Jack said, "getting a ball from Cam would have been No. 1 on the list. It's something I will remember for the rest of my life."

THE PHOTO SHOOT

I found the kids for our photo shoot by mentioning I was looking for them several times in my stories for the *Observer* and online in my blog. We invited them to the newspaper and to Bank of America Stadium on Monday. All they were told was that we would be taking a group picture of the kids and that I would interview all of them.

Meanwhile, we quietly invited Newton, too. His visit on the day after the 17-13 win against New Orleans was a surprise to the kids until I told them a few minutes beforehand so we could start getting set up for the photo.

Although I had asked Newton only to stay for five minutes for a photo, he stayed for 30. Newton invited his own parents, and they came, too.

If you have ever seen Newton with children, you know he is fully in his element. He has a younger brother named Caylin, who is in the ninth grade and also plays football, which probably helps. Around kids, Newton is engaging, funny, self-deprecating and not the least bit intimidating.

Adults have not always accepted him as completely. Newton occasionally was a "bad teammate" by his own admission as a rookie, when he sometimes retreated into self-absorbed sulking under a Gatorade towel when things were going poorly. His coach, Ron Rivera, once jokingly referred to him as "Mr. Mopeyhead." His exaggerated histrionics after first downs and touchdowns sometimes have been criticized by old-school football fans who would prefer no celebrations at all.

Some of Newton's teammates talked to him early about the need to lead better when things were going badly, and he has taken that lesson to heart. This NFL season, his third, he was voted by his teammates as a captain for the first time.

As for kids — they inherently "get" Newton. And he gets them, too. That's why his charity efforts concentrate on children.

Newton has done far more in the Charlotte area than give away a few footballs for kids. Through the School Pride

An ecstatic fan celebrates after receiving a ball from Cam Newton during the Panthers' December 2014 road win over the Saints in New Orleans.
(Observer Photo/Jeff Siner)

partner school program, the Cam Newton Foundation has donated over $225,000 to six local middle schools over the past two years. The foundation also hosted a School Pride day at Memorial Stadium in 2013 attended by nearly 800 students and teachers, and will do another one this coming May. It hosts a seven-on-seven high school football tournament each summer in Charlotte and recently put on "Cam's Thanksgiving Jam," an event that provided food to more than 1,100 local needy families. And there's much more.

On Monday — as with all child-centered events where Newton shows up — the kids sensed that this 24-year-old quarterback who pretends he's an airplane before every game still has a lot of kid in him. They applauded when he came in, then chattered excitedly to him about holiday Twinkies, where he got his shoes and what they wanted for Christmas.

One child proclaimed to the quarterback that the Grinch wasn't real. Another guessed Newton's age to be 300.

'MISS VIRGINIA? I'M CAM'

Newton dazzled all of the parents and all of the kids — except one. The youngest child we could find who ever received a football from Newton was Virginia Brooks, who was 3 when she got it and is 4 now. She was standing in front of Newton in a Panthers cheerleader outfit for the photo. No matter how he tried to entice her, she wouldn't turn around.

"Virginia?" he said. "Miss Virginia? I'm Cam. What's your name?"

No dice. Virginia stayed staring straight ahead, her back to Newton.

"Miss Virginia is literally giving me a cold shoulder," Newton said with a laugh.

Then it was time for all the kids to pose like Superman alongside Newton. He coached them on proper technique first.

"Listen now, this might be the only time you'd be able to scream," Newton said. "Because when I do it, I scream, because a lot of excitement comes out. So on the count of three, we're going to do it and we're going to scream at the camera."

A couple of the kids giggled.

"I don't laugh when I do it now," Newton said, putting on a fake stern face. "This ain't no joke. This is the real deal. Superman! Right here! All right. You ready? Everybody ready? You ready, Miss Virginia? One. Two. Three!!!!"

The howl after "three" might have been heard in New Orleans. It sent Virginia scurrying out of the picture setup and into the arms of her mother.

Newton, who had gotten permission from Virginia's parents to hold her in his lap if she would agree, instead found himself grasping at air as she bolted the scene.

Virginia would make a quick recovery, though. When I asked Virginia that day how she and her brother Turner had gotten a ball, she said:

"Cam scored a touchdown. He gave me and my brother the ball. We keep it in my brother's room. And we have a dog named Sadie."

As for Newton, he eventually had to go. He signed everyone's touchdown ball first with a silver Sharpie. Then he rose up, with the children by this time following him around like the Pied Piper.

Virginia smiled at him. Hannah twirled her football. Miles Bolin kept doing the Superman pose. Sebastian Cortez asked for Newton to sign his football a second time, which the quarterback did.

Like he has done so many times already in the Carolinas, Newton had taken some of his free time and used it to positively affect a bunch of kids.

"Keep sleeping with those pigs," Newton teased.

And then Cam Newton finally had to go to a meeting with his coaches as he tried to figure out how to get the team into the end zone more often and ultimately give away more of those footballs.

The quarterback walked back into the dark tunnels underneath the Panthers' stadium, leaving behind a bright memory that 15 children will never forget. ★

Cam Newton strikes his Superman pose with a group of children who have received a football from the quarterback following a Panthers touchdown. (Observer Photo/Jeff Siner)

Newton: 'God Has Hands on Me'

Two Days after Scary Wreck, Panthers Star Quarterback Says He's Thankful to Be Alive

By Joseph Person | December 12, 2014

Carolina Panthers quarterback Cam Newton says he's not worried about when he might play again. He's just thankful to be alive.

Speaking for the first time since he was injured in a two-car crash in uptown Charlotte, Newton repeatedly mentioned his good fortune in escaping the wreck with two fractures in his lower back.

"I'm on somebody's fantasy league, and I think it's the man upstairs," Newton said at Bank of America Stadium.

Newton was back at the stadium less than 48 hours after his lunchtime wreck left his black pickup truck totaled and ignited a social media frenzy as Panthers fans and NFL followers sought updates on his condition.

"I really couldn't talk afterward because I was in such shock," Newton said. "I got myself out of the truck, and I couldn't stop smiling.

"I'm looking at this truck and I'm like, 'Somebody's supposed to be dead.' And I just can't stop smiling because it's like, God has his hands on me."

After spending Tuesday night at Carolinas Medical Center, Newton was released Wednesday and returned to the stadium Thursday to receive treatment and attend meetings with the team's other quarterbacks.

He will sit out Sunday's home game against the Tampa Bay Buccaneers, just the second game he will have missed since the Panthers selected him with the No. 1 pick in the 2011 NFL draft.

Dallas Cowboys quarterback Tony Romo sustained the same injury as Newton's — two transverse process fractures — this season and returned after missing one game. Panthers coach Ron Rivera said Thursday is the best-case scenario for

Top: Police and fire officials examine Cam Newton's 1998 Dodge Ram following the December 9, 2014, accident. (Observer Photo/Todd Sumlin)

Bottom: A Charlotte firefighter tends to Newton. (Observer Photos/Todd Sumlin)

Newton to return in time for the Dec. 21 game against Cleveland.

But Newton said concerns about his football status are secondary.

"As far as when I'm coming back, who cares? That's not something that I'm worried about right now," Newton said. "I'm just thankful to have breath in my lungs."

Newton said he never lost consciousness during the wreck, which occurred at the intersection of South Church and West Hill streets, a block from the Panthers' stadium.

Newton was traveling south on Church when he said he saw the driver of the other vehicle, Nestor Pellot Jr., pull out and attempt to cross Church in a Buick sedan. Newton said he attempted to avoid Pellot's car, but the Buick "clipped the back of my truck."

The impact of the collision caused Newton's truck to overturn on the bridge over the John Belk Freeway.

Neither driver was cited in the crash, which happened at Charlotte's fourth-most dangerous intersection, according to traffic statistics.

Newton, 25, was traveling at the posted speed limit of 35 mph at the time of the accident, according to the crash report.

Newton said the airbags deployed in his truck, and he sustained no external cuts or injuries. He climbed out of the rear window of the truck, then sat on a curb while emergency personnel checked him out.

The crash report shows Newton's truck sustained $9,000 in damage, while Pellot's 2013 Buick had $4,000 in damage.

Pellot, 46, was treated and released at Novant Health Presbyterian Medical Center.

Newton, who wore a blue hoodie and leaned on a lectern during his seven-minute press conference, said he came to the stadium Thursday in part to ease the minds of teammates and coaches.

Rivera said Newton looked "a little sore" but otherwise appeared to be OK.

"When he gets warmed up and treated, he moves around pretty good. He's in good spirits. He's positive," Rivera said. "There's a lot for him to build on as we go forward and see what happens in a week or so, as far as his health is concerned."

When Newton saw Panthers cornerback Josh Norman on Thursday, Newton jokingly told him he needed to intercept more passes.

With his overturned truck nearby following the accident on Church Street, Cam Newton is treated by firefighters. (Observer Photo/Todd Sumlin)

The 2013 Buick that collided with Cam Newton's truck sustained $4,000 in damage.

"I said, 'Well we need you back so you can throw the ball more,'" Norman said. "It's one of those joking things, playing with him. He's in good spirits overall."

Newton said he didn't want his situation to become a distraction for the Panthers as they prepare for a Tampa Bay team that is 2-11 and has been eliminated from playoff contention.

The Panthers (4-8-1), despite going more than two months between victories before last week's 41-10 win at New Orleans, are just a half-game behind the Saints (5-8) and Atlanta (5-8) for first place in the NFC South.

Backup quarterback Derek Anderson will fill in for Newton against the Buccaneers, as he did during a Week 1 win at Tampa Bay when Newton was sidelined with cracked ribs.

"I'm looking forward to seeing Bank of America (stadium) as hyped as it's been this whole year," Newton said. "I'm anticipating a big win for these guys, and I'm backing D.A. 100 percent."

Newton said seeing pictures of his 1998 Dodge Ram, with its smashed cab on the passenger's side, made him realize how fortunate he was.

"I'm just lucky to come out of there unscathed with just the little injury that I did have," Newton said. "Every time I see that flashback of looking at that truck, I'm surprised that nothing serious was done to me." ✪

Newton, Norman Fight at Training Camp

Newton: Why All the Fuss about Fight?

By Joseph Person | August 12, 2015

A calm settled over the Carolina Panthers' training camp Tuesday, a day after the $103 million franchise quarterback fought the team's top cornerback.

Following an incident-free practice that featured no discernible trash talking, quarterback Cam Newton sought to defuse the situation with Josh Norman by saying there was no bad blood between the two players.

Newton expressed no regrets about Monday's fight and said the incident would serve to make the team stronger. He also dismissed the idea that, as the Panthers' franchise quarterback and biggest investment, he needs to avoid situations that put him at a risk of injury.

"I think we're making a big deal out of nothing," Newton said. "It's no need for me to tell you guys what happened outside of we are better because of it.

"After speaking with the team, after guys coming up and approaching, it's a lot of things that was said that was in the moment. I've seen the video that people posted. But at the end of the day, it's not for the world to know what the Carolina Panthers are doing."

About 10 minutes after Newton finished with the media, news broke that New York Jets quarterback Geno Smith would be sidelined 6-to-10 weeks with a broken jaw after being sucker punched by a teammate in the locker room.

If Smith's jaw didn't underscore what might have happened to Norman or Newton had the fight carried into the locker room or the Wofford dorms, it at least removed the Panthers from Position A in the 24-hour sports news cycle.

Cam Newton's fight with cornerback Josh Norman during training camp in 2015 was national news. "I think we're making a big deal out of nothing," Newton said a day after the incident. (Observer Photo/David T. Foster III)

The outspoken Norman was not made available to the media for the second day in a row.

And while Norman and Newton had jawed throughout the first week of training camp, Newton said there are no hard feelings between the two. He said reporters only see their exchanges on the field.

"Of course I'm not going to say, 'Hey, Josh your cleats are cool.' No. You don't see when I'm talking to Josh right here," Newton said. "You don't see when I'm talking to Josh in the dorms. So of course you guys are going to report of course Cam doesn't like Josh.

"I see this guy every day. I've seen that No. 24 has become better and better each

and every year. And I know I have a feeling this will be his best year yet."

Newton threw in Norman's direction several times Tuesday. He completed a couple of the passes, Norman broke one up and another sailed over the head of Kelvin Benjamin, who was covered well by Norman.

Norman came up toward Newton on a scramble, but coaches blew the play dead before any contact was made. There was no chirping between them.

As he did at the start of camp when addressing questions about his offseason activities, which included participating in an Aussie rules football trip and playing in a flag football tournament, Newton said he

Cam Newton and Josh Norman jawed throughout the first week of training camp in 2015. (Observer Photo/David T. Foster III)

wouldn't succumb to public pressure about how he leads his life.

Asked if he would do it again, Newton said: "Do what again? Practice hard? Yes, I practice hard each and every day. I have no regrets of things that I've done."

He also outlined what he intends to do next.

"What's the blueprint of a franchise quarterback? Leading your team," Newton said. "I'm not going to let no one dictate how I play. I'm not going to let no one dictate how I feel."

Panthers coaches and players were ready to move on from the fight Tuesday.

Tight end Greg Olsen scoffed at the notion that the 6-foot-5 Newton risked getting hurt in the fracas with Norman, who's 6 feet tall and 195 pounds.

"I think everyone needs to stop overreacting," Olsen said. "He's 265 pounds. He could be 275 pounds if he wanted to. He's one of the biggest guys on the team. He carries the ball 15 times a game like a running back. I think a little hand-slapping fight with a DB in practice, I think we'll be OK."

Panthers coach Ron Rivera said he didn't "put the kibosh" on trash-talking, adding that players likely realized they needed to tone it down.

"Obviously, (Monday) wasn't a good situation for us, and as far as I'm concerned the situation's over," Rivera said. "If it goes on, I'll address it as it happens."

New contract or otherwise, Newton doesn't plan to change, including his approach to practice.

He'll continue to trade playful barbs with linebacker Thomas Davis, run from drill

to drill and, if he has to, get in a shoving match with a defensive back who stiff-arms him after an interception.

"I know you guys want to make a story about the scuffle. And 'We've never seen a franchise quarterback involved...'" Newton said. "Yeah, but there's a lot of what I do that is not prototypical. You know what I'm saying? We have fun. I enjoy doing what I do. And that approach gets me the enjoyment from practice." ✪

"I think everyone needs to stop overreacting," said Panthers tight end Greg Olsen the day after a shoving match between quarterback Cam Newton and cornerback Josh Norman. (Observer Photo/David T. Foster III)

NOT OLD ENOUGH TO GET THAT CALL

In his four-plus years in the NFL, Carolina Panthers quarterback Cam Newton had absorbed some hits that may be considered late hits to smaller, less mobile quarterbacks.

In a 27-22 victory over New Orleans in 2015, he took a similar hit that drew no flag. But the reason he got for the no-call didn't have to do with his 6-foot-5, 255-pound frame.

It had to do with his age.

"I was really baffled by what was said to me," Newton said after the game in his news conference. "I was rolling out trying to string out the play and create some type of opportunity to get a completion and the defensive lineman, you know, kind of hit me. It was close. It was right on the cusp. Was it a late hit? I don't know. But the response that I got was, 'Cam you're not old enough to get that call.'"

Those words allegedly came from the NFL's most popular referee, Ed Hochuli. A source close to Hochuli said the referee denied making the statement to Newton.

The Panthers had the ball at their 12 early in the fourth quarter when the hit came. Out of the shotgun on first down, Newton rolled to his right to buy time looking for tight end Greg Olsen down the field.

Saints defensive tackle Tyeler Davison gave chase and hit Newton around the time he released the pass, knocking the quarterback to the ground in front of referee Hochuli.

Newton looked to Hochuli, and upon getting a response, Newton could be seen shaking his head demonstratively in a show of disagreement.

"If he would have said he missed the call, that's one thing," Newton said. "But for his response to be what it was, that I'm not old enough to get that call, geez. So heaven forbid he gets any rookies. They're going to have a long day. So, I don't know."

—Joseph Person and Jonathan Jones

CAM
MOMENT

Victories Define Cam's Greatness

How Should Carolina Panthers QB Cam Newton Be Measured? By Wins, He Says

By Joseph Person | September 5, 2015

Cam Newton is tired of people telling him what he can't do.

Through his first four NFL seasons, the Carolina Panthers' franchise quarterback couldn't open a web browser without reading about his deficiencies as a pocket passer, a leader of men and a reader of defenses.

Newton broke Peyton Manning's rookie passing record (since broken again by Andrew Luck) after the Panthers drafted him No. 1 in 2011. He's been to two Pro Bowls and took the Panthers to the playoffs in back-to-back years for the first time in their history.

But the storylines surrounding Newton weren't his rocket right arm or running ability, but his overthrown passes and sideline demeanor.

Some of the criticism is warranted: Newton's career 59.5 completion percentage lags well behind those of NFC South rivals Drew Brees (66.2) and Matt Ryan (64.0). Panthers backup quarterback Derek Anderson is only a 53.7 percent career passer, but he completed 66.2 percent of his throws last season in two starts against Tampa Bay.

The criticism extended to Newton's off-the-field activities this summer after he signed a $103.8 million contract extension, the most lucrative ever given to a Panthers player.

Fans and media members chastised the newly minted Newton for risking injury by participating in an Aussie Rules Football practice during a Gatorade tour of Australia and playing a couple of snaps in a flag football tournament in Atlanta.

There were more questions last month after Newton fought with Panthers cornerback Josh Norman during a training camp practice.

Cam Newton celebrates after the Panthers' playoff win over the defending NFC champion Seattle Seahawks in January 2016. (Observer Photo/David T. Foster III)

Newton responded by saying he's not like other quarterbacks and he wouldn't allow the public to put him in a box.

During an interview with the *Observer* last week, Newton expanded on his camp comments about playing quarterback and living life by his own standards and measures.

"I've always had that somewhat alpha approach. We play in a league where you have to get yourself going in a rather unique way," Newton said while walking back to Bank of America Stadium after practice. "But I never want anyone to play this game and feel obligated to be a robot. I think so much in society is morphing people into what they want rather than what the actual person wants to be."

THE SAME GOAL

What Newton wants first and foremost is to be a champion. Ask him about his goals for this season — any season — and he says, "Always, win the Super Bowl."

Newton has a losing record (30-31-1) as a starter since entering the league after winning a national championship and Heisman Trophy at Auburn. But he won a playoff game for the first time last season and got the huge contract because the Panthers believe he can lead them to the "promised land," as general manager Dave Gettleman said.

Anderson says Newton's style is "not always going to be pretty … or going to be what all the analysts want to see."

But Anderson has seen Newton develop into a more complete quarterback over his first four seasons. And not even Newton's harshest critics can question his desire to win.

"Wins and losses in football go on the quarterback and head coach. That's one thing that irks him more than anything, or drives him to be better," Anderson said. "And he's definitely a guy when the game's on the line, he's focused. He wants the ball. He's going to make plays for us. … I never have any doubt when the bullets are flying he's going to be ready."

PANTHERS GO ATYPICAL

Ronde Barber, the former Tampa Bay cornerback who's now a Fox game analyst, said not every organization would have drafted Newton, preferring a prototypical pocket passer as their franchise quarterback.

But Barber credits Panthers coach Ron Rivera and offensive coordinator Mike Shula for using a scheme that best suits Newton's talents.

"There's not a lot of teams that want a guy like Cam to be their franchise quarterback. They want the other type - the big pocket passers, guys that can control a game and keep the ball moving," Barber said in a recent interview.

"Cam is so unique … and I feel like Mike Shula and Ron really embrace who he is instead of trying to make him one of those other guys. And I think last year that started to show."

The Panthers looked for ways to capitalize on Newton's unique skill set even before drafting him. Former offensive coordinator Rob Chudzinski studied Auburn's offense and incorporated

Panthers quarterbacks coach Mike Shula talks with Cam Newton during the fourth quarter of the Panthers' October 2012 loss to the Bears in Chicago. (Observer Photo/Jeff Siner)

elements of the zone read, which Shula still uses effectively.

"That thought process for us came in April his first year," Shula said. "Whether or not we wanted to draft him, and why, and what we knew about him and how he was wired and how to get the best out of him."

Newton has thrived as a runner, be it on a zone-read play, a scramble or a quarterback keeper at the goal line.

During a 2014 season in which he missed two games — the first of his NFL career — with rib and back injuries, Newton picked up first downs on 43.7 percent of his

Panthers tight end Greg Olsen hugs Cam Newton during practice at Wofford College on July 31, 2015. (Observer Photo/Jeff Siner)

rushing attempts, the best percentage in the league.

Newton is the first player in NFL history to gain 10,000 passing yards and 2,000 rushing yards in his first four seasons, and joined Randall Cunningham and Michael Vick as the only quarterbacks with four or more 500-yard rushing seasons.

Newton is listed at 6-foot-5 and 245 pounds, although Panthers tight end Greg Olsen said this summer Newton's playing weight is closer to 260.

His size, speed and elusiveness make Newton a load to bring down. Consider that since 2011, Newton has more rushing touchdowns than all but three running backs.

"He's a different breed, that's for sure," Anderson said. "He's not your typical quarterback who we're used to seeing coming through the '80s and '90s. He's kind of the new wave of athlete, probably your best athlete on the field at times. And he's going to do things a little more unorthodox than people maybe want.

"But our goal is to make sure we're refining those things — mechanically, pocket presence, all that sort of stuff, which I think he's gotten a heck of a lot better at."

GROWTH AND TEMPO

Newton's improved ability to read defenses and make the appropriate pre-snap checks coincided with Shula's increased use of the no-huddle last season.

Newton says the hurry-up allows him to quickly survey the defense and get the Panthers into favorable plays and matchups.

"The more that you see, the better off you will be," Newton said. "It's not anything worth panicking about when we are in that type of tempo. It is tempoing just enough for us to play fast and have the defense hesitate somewhat."

Anderson said Newton has become better at recognizing disguised coverages and blitzes, regardless of whether the Panthers are huddling or running their hurry-up attack.

"The things we're doing give him a little more freedom at times. But also he gets in a flow, I feel like, be it no-huddle or coming out of the huddle," Anderson said. "I think he's doing a great job at both of them, which I think early on in his career he'd even tell you, he struggled a little bit. But I think it also just comes from growth in general."

Newton faced a steeper learning curve than a quarterback like the Colts' Luck, who spent three seasons in Stanford's pro-style offense before the Colts drafted him No. 1 in 2012. Newton started only one season at a four-year school, directing an Auburn spread offense in which plays were signaled by hand.

Anderson said Newton faced an adjustment period calling plays in the huddle, especially with the NFL's complicated verbiage. But Shula has seen Newton grow more comfortable with the entire offense, including the no-huddle.

"That doesn't mean we're going to go no-huddle all the time. We're going to mix it in like we've done," Shula said. "Just seeing how defenses are disguising things, I think he's got a better feel for that. But it's a learning (process) every year."

'STILL OFF TARGET SOMETIMES'

But there are still areas where Newton can improve.

His 82.1 passer rating last season was the worst of his career and ranked 26th among 33 qualified quarterbacks.

Shula said he'd like to see Newton, who has a 59.5 career completion percentage, be closer to the mid-60s. Shula said the Panthers can help Newton by being more productive on first and second downs and staying out of third-and-longs.

But some observers believe Newton will always struggle with his accuracy, particularly the high throws he has become known for. Drafting a pair of tall receivers in Kelvin Benjamin and Devin Funchess the past two years should help, although Benjamin tore his ACL during camp and is out for the season.

"He's still going to have the errant throws and the ball's going to come out high. He's still off target sometimes," said Barber, the Fox analyst. "But I think they understand that about him now. They play to his strengths a lot better."

The Panthers' receivers have struggled since Benjamin's injury. In the third exhibition against New England, Newton

Cam Newton takes a photograph with fans following Fan Fest at Bank of America Stadium on August 7, 2015. (Observer Photo/Jeff Siner)

completed 17 of 28 passes for 160 yards and a touchdown. Still, his rating of 88.4 was nearly 30 points higher than Tom Brady's.

But Newton's numbers would have been better if not for at least five drops by his receivers.

The lack of a play-making replacement for Benjamin and the shaky performance by the receiving corps during the preseason begs a familiar question: Does Newton have enough weapons?

"I don't have any choice. The answers are in the locker room," he said after the Patriots exhibition. "It is not up to me. I have full confidence in the personnel, I've got full confidence in myself."

How should Newton be measured?

After Newton's fight with Norman in Spartanburg, a reporter mentioned that most quarterbacks don't get into those types of scraps with teammates.

"Says who? You've never seen a guy in a red jersey like me," said Newton, referring to the practice jerseys worn by the Panthers quarterbacks.

"I know you guys want to make a story about the scuffle and, 'We've never seen a franchise quarterback involved …'

"Yeah, but there's a lot of what I do that is not prototypical. You know what I'm saying?"

Olsen does.

The Panthers' Pro Bowl tight end thought the media made too much of Newton's training camp fight, but said that's been the case with whatever Newton has done throughout his career.

"People can't seem to get over trying to put Cam into a box and judge every move and every facial expression, him sitting on a bench, the way he walks, the way he talks," Olsen said last month. "We're going into Year 5 now. I think that storyline both locally and nationally is played out. I think guys are tired of answering it. I'm sure he's tired of answering it."

Once the regular-season games start the questions will involve Newton's decisions and throws, what he saw on a particular play, and, ultimately, what went right or wrong for the Panthers in 2015.

How will Newton measure up?

"I guess we'll see," Newton said, reiterating the Super Bowl is his top goal. "But we have to put actions to (work), and not talk about it." ✪

Cam Newton celebrates after Carolina defeated Seattle to advance to the NFC Championship Game in January 2016. (Observer Photo/David T. Foster III)

CAM MOMENT

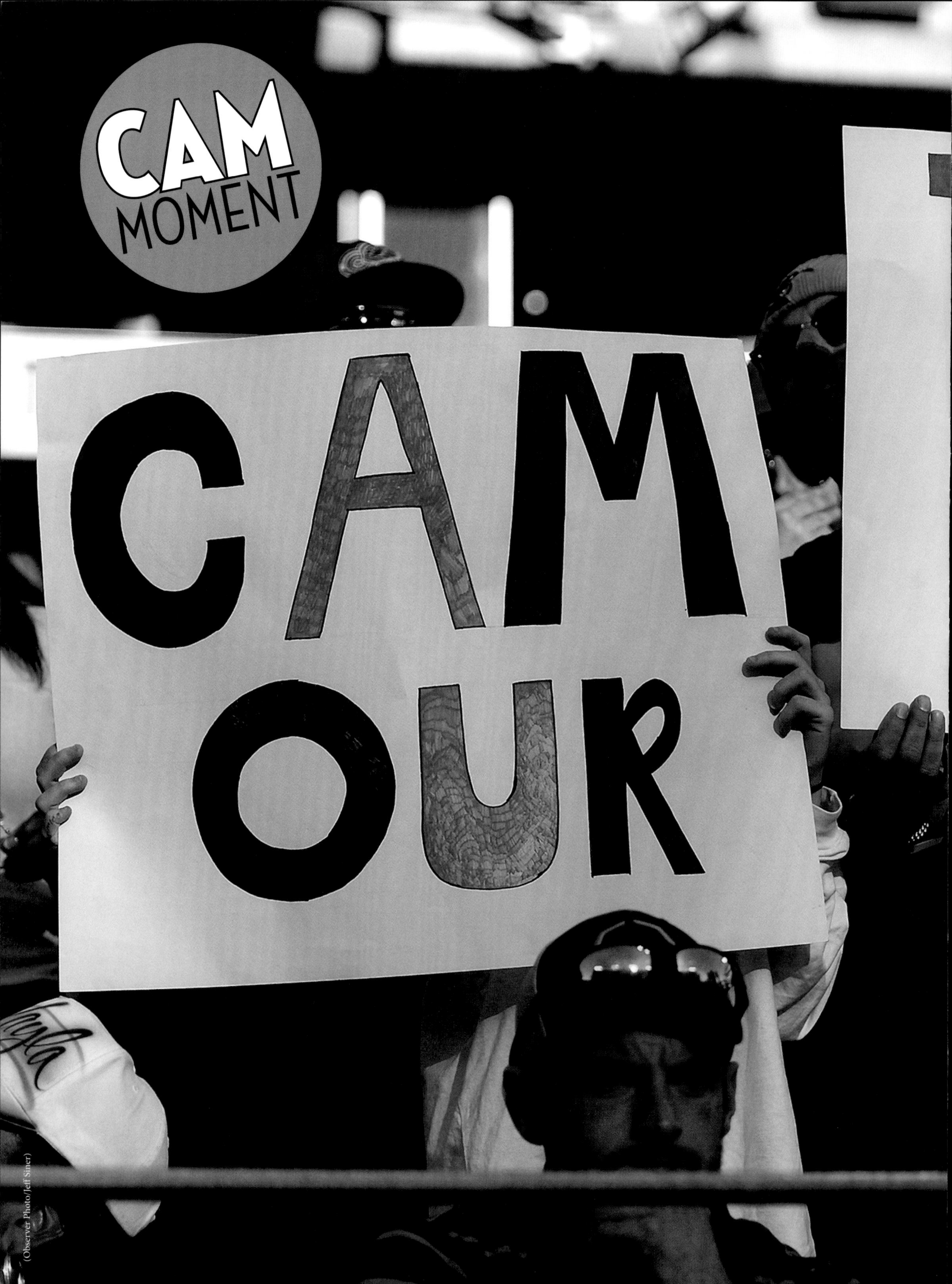

(Observer Photo/Jeff Siner)

THE PACKERS BANNER

A Green Bay Packers fan had his team banner snatched down by Cam Newton during the 2015 season and reported the incident to police as a theft. He said he expected the Panthers to "make it right."

As a result, the fan got angry messages, even death threats.

Mike Dobs, an Army veteran who lives in Fayetteville, said Newton ran up and snatched the banner "out of our hands" before the game against the Packers in Charlotte.

"We thought it was a joke at first, but he never came back with the banner," Dobs said. "That's when I went to security and told them he stole it. The first officer I talked to just laughed."

Dobs' banner had a green map of North Carolina with the Green Bay logo in the middle and the words "North Carolina Cheesehead," referring to the nickname Green Bay fans give themselves.

Newton said after the game that he grabbed the banner and explained that he felt it was disrespectful to Panthers fans and their home, Bank of America Stadium.

At a news conference, Rivera referred to the incident as a "side story." However, he said he wished Newton had not done it.

"It's still a side story, as far as I'm concerned," he said. "It's being taken care of. Cam's been talked to, and we are reaching out to the other party. That's where we are."

—Mark Price

Head Over Heels

Cam Newton's Flipping TD Was a Stunner

By Scott Fowler | September 21, 2015

Oh no, he didn't!

Oh yes, he did.

That was the collective reaction Sunday at Bank of America Stadium when Carolina Panthers quarterback Cam Newton made one of the most spectacular plays of his NFL career, scoring on a 2-yard quarterback draw by doing a full front flip into the end zone over a hapless defender.

It was the most gasp-inducing moment of an uneven but ultimately successful Sunday for the Panthers, who edged Houston 24-17 in their home opener to move to 2-0.

"My heart was in my socks," Newton said of the play. "As I was flipping, I was like, 'Hey, I wonder how this is going to end?' And then I'm coming down and said, 'Hey, I can stick this!'"

Those kinds of plays are why Carolina signed Newton to a $103 million contract extension in the offseason. Newton accounted for all three Carolina touchdowns Sunday — throwing perfect strikes of 25 yards to Ted Ginn Jr. and 36 yards to Philly Brown for the other two.

But it was the flip that everyone was flipping out about later.

"He's probably the only quarterback in the league who can do that," Panthers tight end Greg Olsen said. "That's obvious. When you have a quarterback run designed for the goal line, and you block everybody but the one guy you can't block, and then the quarterback jumps over him, it's hard to game plan for that."

Said Ginn: "You don't see a lot of guys 6-foot-6 who are that athletic who play football. You see them play basketball or run track or something. For a guy to be a quarterback and to do something I can't do is amazing."

To be fair, Newton ultimately did not stick the landing. Although he hurdled free safety Rahim Moore cleanly, while in the air he was hit by defensive end Jared Crick. He came down a bit awkwardly on a

Cam Newton smiles after flipping through the air to cross the goal line against Houston in September 2015. (Observer Photo/Jeff Siner)

Cam Newton goes upside down and airborne to score a third-quarter touchdown against the Houston Texans. (Observer Photo/Jeff Siner)

foot and a knee before springing up and doing his Superman celebration.

It was especially appropriate this time, since he had just finished flying.

"Superman, huh?" Panthers cornerback Josh Norman said. "He went up and over and almost landed on his feet! Hey that's our guy."

Said Olsen of Newton: "I told him the Russian judge gave him a 3, but everyone else gave him a 10."

Center Ryan Kalil was right next to Newton, but was blocking and didn't see the flip live. When Kalil came to the sideline, though, and heard the buzz that wouldn't stop throughout the stands and listened to teammates saying, "You have to see this," he looked up at the scoreboard replay. He was awed like everyone else.

I had an exchange with Newton in his press conference after the game that went like this.

Q. Why did you flip over the safety instead of trying to run him over?

A. "Well, I think you would have had something to say if I tried to run him over, too."

Q. But wasn't the degree of difficulty higher on a flip?

A. "Well, not necessarily. My thinking is there's an imaginary line right there, and if I cross the plane with it, with the ball, it's a touchdown. Flip, no flip, fumble, no fumble, as long as I get across the plane with the ball. ... I kind of eyed the safety and he was gearing up, scrunching his face like that (Newton then made a squinty face). I didn't want to read in *The Charlotte Observer* the next day that Cam has to be smarter running. So I just gave you all an extra thing to write about."

That he did, and put in a plug for the newspaper as well. Thanks for both, Cam.

Newton threw for 195 yards Sunday, ran for 76 and overcame several key dropped passes (again) for a victory.

As for the flip itself: It only tied at No. 1 for the best flip Newton has ever done in the NFL.

In 2012, he finished a 72-yard touchdown run against Atlanta with another front somersault into the end zone. The one Sunday was over a defender intent on inflicting harm; the one three years ago was just a giddy celebration of making it into the end zone.

On the other hand, the 72-yarder came after running at a full sprint for most of the field. In terms of difficulty, I would rate them as evenly impossible for anybody like you or me.

"I always wanted a trampoline," Newton said.

On Sunday, he invented his own. ✪

Cam Newton and Panthers coach Ron Rivera bow their heads during a moment of silence in remembrance of the victims of the Paris terrorist attacks, before the Panthers' November 15, 2015, game against the Tennessee Titans in Nashville. (Observer Photo/Jeff Siner)

A Complete Football Player

Newton Plays Best as Leader

By Scott Fowler | October 20, 2015

Cam Newton has always been a great athlete.

On Sunday, he was a great football player.

In Carolina's 27-23 comeback victory at Seattle, what you saw in the final eight minutes was a quarterback playing the position as well as he has ever played it. That was as close to perfect as Newton has ever been.

I watched the last two drives again on Monday, and here is what I saw. Newton threw a 25-yard strike to Devin Funchess that Funchess managed to drop. He spiked the ball once to kill the clock.

And other than that, he went 11-for-11.

Running? It wasn't even part of the equation for Newton.

Was Greg Olsen just bailing him out over and over? No.

Here are Newton's last six passes of the game, in order (not including the spike):

Eight yards to Jonathan Stewart.

Eighteen yards to Ted Ginn.

Fourteen yards to Ed Dickson.

Sixteen yards to Funchess.

Seven yards to Jerricho Cotchery.

And, finally, 26 yards to Olsen for the game-winning TD.

Six completions. Six different receivers. In a storm of noise. And all without his No. 1 wide receiver, Kelvin Benjamin.

Richard Sherman called the winning touchdown pass to Olsen a "fluky play" since the Seahawks got confused on their coverage and left Olsen wide open.

But what Newton did on Sunday? That was no fluke. That was the continuing maturation of one of the NFL's best quarterbacks.

That is what the Panthers gave Newton that huge contract to do. Early in his career, he had all kinds of trouble completing fourth-quarter comebacks — even though he usually had a better corps of receivers to throw the ball to then he does at the moment. He would try too often for the big

Cam Newton fends off an Atlanta defender during a December 2011 Panthers loss to the Falcons. Newton set the NFL's single-season rushing record for a quarterback during his rookie season in 2011. (Observer Photo/David T. Foster III)

play, and then the big mistake would come instead.

Early in his career, that moment after the sack vs. Seattle that Newton took on the final drive that pushed the Panthers into a second-and-19? That would have been the beginning of the end.

Not anymore. Now Newton is doing an amazing job for these 5-0 Carolina Panthers. On a team that lacks offensive explosion, he led four 80-yard touchdown drives — four! — on Sunday. On the road. Against a team that has made the Super Bowl the past two years.

I would rank No. 1 as the No. 3 quarterback in the NFL right now, trailing only Aaron Rodgers and Tom Brady. You can make a number of arguments against that, of course. But I look at Newton's supporting cast and I look at how he has limited his mistakes and I don't think he has ever had a longer, more consistent stretch of good play.

Said linebacker Thomas Davis following the win about Newton: "I think he's going to start getting some of the respect that he deserves as one of the best quarterbacks in the league, a guy that can flat-out lead the team and go out there and get it done. He's going to erase some of the doubters that he has. We're excited to have him as our quarterback."

Said coach Ron Rivera of Newton on Monday: "I thought Cam made some really good decisions, especially in the fourth quarter."

Said Newton after the game of the winning drive: "I don't want to make this

Cam Newton is all smiles after Jonathan Stewart's first-quarter touchdown against the Seattle Seahawks in January 2016. Carolina won the NFC divisional playoff game, 31-24. (Observer Photo/David T. Foster III)

about me. It was a great team win, and an unbelievable catch by Greg. Just an unbelievable game by him, being there when I needed him the most."

Certainly, Olsen was phenomenal. The Panthers came into the game dead last in the NFL in number of offensive plays of 20 or more yards. They had a respectable four Sunday, and Newton-to-Olsen passes accounted for all four.

And it truly wasn't all about Cam. Other than that one sack, the Panthers' offensive line protected beautifully on the last two marches. Cotchery made a third-down catch in worse traffic than what you find at 5 p.m. on I-485. Funchess, who dropped three balls during the game, made a leaping grab in the final minutes. Olsen was, well, Olsen.

"Yeah, they just made some plays," Seattle coach Pete Carroll said. "We were able to pressure him at times in there and get some balls thrown away, but he had enough."

Yes, Newton had enough. For the first time in five tries against Seattle, despite two nasty interceptions earlier in the game, Newton had more than enough.

Newton made it sound businesslike after the game concluded.

"Well, we were just doing our job," he said. "Nothing special. They're a good team. We're a good team, too."

But you could tell what his true reaction to this win was right after that touchdown, when Cam went screaming and jumping to the sideline.

This was a huge game in Newton's development. He knows this. And in the wake of that comeback from 13 points down, nothing seems out of reach for a team that has a quarterback playing like that. ✪

Above: Fans at Bank of America Stadium celebrate the Panthers' January 2016 win over the Seattle Seahawks.

Opposite: Cam Newton scrambles away from Saints defenders during Carolina's December 2013 win over New Orleans. (Observer Photos/Jeff Siner)

CAM MOMENT

ROCK THE BABY

Newton left the Panthers' Christmas Eve 2015 practice five plays early to get to Atlanta, where he is from and where Chosen Sebastian Newton was born. He then came back to Charlotte for a Saturday practice before returning to Atlanta, where he and the Panthers lost for the first time all season to the Atlanta Falcons.

Newton's best moment in that game came when he scored on a touchdown run in the first quarter. He then pretended the football was a baby and that he was rocking it to sleep, although after the game he wouldn't answer a question as to why he did that.

The following Thursday, when he finally answered the questions, it was easy to remember that Newton is only 26. He sounded naive, for instance, when answering a question about what the past week has been like.

"Yeah, I had a child," he said. "The people who needed to know have known for awhile. Nothing has pretty much changed besides our record, and the focus now is still the same. There were a lot of distractions last week — and the main one was probably the practice schedule more than anything."

As Newton will soon find out, everything has changed.

You are not a father, and then suddenly you are. That's the big leap.

—Scott Fowler

Newton's Moves Not Out of Step

Explaining Newton's Touchdown Celebration

By Jonathan Jones | November 17, 2015

The explanation of Cam Newton's touchdown celebration in Sunday's victory against the Tennessee Titans is simple, but complex.

Newton is a young, successful black man celebrating through culturally relevant means.

It's not hard to grasp that concept, though talk radio callers and a half-dozen Panthers fans who have emailed me have struggled to do so. Let's unfold it.

In the fourth quarter of Sunday's 27-10 victory in Nashville, Tenn., Newton extended the ball across the goal line for his sixth rushing touchdown of the season. As is his wont, he found an unoccupied spot in the end zone where he could put his dance moves on display.

First came a few dance steps and then the dab, a dance move born in Atlanta and Googled across Charlotte since Sunday afternoon. He followed that up with another dance step, "hittin' dem folks" once, and then did it twice more in the faces of Titans defenders displeased with his celebrations.

Titans interim coach Mike Mularkey called it taunting. After the game Newton said he wasn't being boastful; he was just being himself.

Newton is from Atlanta, the unofficial black capital of the United States. Two Saturdays ago I sat at a bar in midtown Atlanta and I was not a minority. Not that I've kept track, but I can't remember that ever happening to me in Charlotte.

Newton carries with him the same culture so heavily influenced by African-Americans. Atlanta birthed Martin Luther King Jr. and OutKast. Newton saw the rise and fall of Michael Vick, the most dynamic quarterback in league history to that point.

Quarterbacks across the NFL celebrate touchdowns. Aaron Rodgers' Discount Double Check move is so loved it's become a commercial. Tom Brady cusses and carries on like he's in a high school cafeteria. Brett

Cam Newton dances in the end zone after rushing for a touchdown late in the fourth quarter against Tennessee on November 15, 2015. The Panthers defeated the Titans 27-10. (Observer Photo/Jeff Siner)

Cam Newton signals for a first down during the fourth quarter of the Panthers' November 2015 win in Nashville. (Observer Photo/Jeff Siner)

Favre, who once did the since-banned throat-slash gesture in a game, would rip off his helmet and run around aimlessly after scores.

So why is Newton any different? He celebrated a touchdown — in a league that features the greatest athletes in the world — by doing a popular dance his little brother asked him to do.

Placed in a vacuum, that story should be one we celebrate.

The great black quarterbacks who came before Newton didn't celebrate — for any number of reasons. Maybe they didn't have rhythm. Maybe they had different temperaments. Or maybe — and probably — they couldn't, for fear of the reaction.

We've seen the kind of fuss Newton's celebration has caused before, when baseball star Ken Griffey Jr. wore his hat backward in the mid-90s.

Black people had played baseball for decades, but Griffey brought the game to generation of kids and made it look fun.

You waggled your bat like Griffey, wore your hat backward like he did in the home run derby. You had your parents buy his signature sneakers, which rarely happened with a baseball player.

In much the same way, Newton is ushering in football for a new generation. He has the 10th-best selling jersey in the country, according to Dick's Sporting Goods. His Superman pose is imitated at every level of the game.

Before Sunday's game, Trenton McNair, son of legendary Tennessee Titans quarterback Steve McNair, was at the game in Nashville, where his father was the NFL's MVP in 2003, four years after he came within a foot of a Super Bowl victory. Trenton could have been in his dad's throwback jersey. Instead he wore a blue No. 1 Panthers jersey, and he spoke with Newton before the game.

Of course Newton's dances are a form of self-aggrandizement. There is an inherent "look at me" nature to any celebration — white or black player, quarterback or otherwise.

But perhaps unwittingly, Newton is introducing a culture foreign to a good portion of Charlotte. Historically, there's resistance when that has happened. Sometimes it's followed by acceptance.

Some people are mad at Newton, and I can assure you he does not care.

Monday morning across Charlotte, people were doing the dab and hittin' dem folks, but only after they tried it in private Sunday night. ✪

Cam Newton holds the ball aloft after rushing for a first down against the Tennessee Titans on November 15, 2015. (Observer Photo/Jeff Siner)

Santa Cam

Newton's Sleigh Stops Across City

By Jonathan Jones | December 16, 2015

The closest Cam Newton ever got to a celebrity before he went to college as a highly touted recruit was at his private elementary school in the mid-1990s.

Atlanta Braves outfielder and three-time All-Star David Justice came to Solid Rock Academy, where Newton was a student, and did little more than a quick cameo.

"It was like, 'All right he's here, say hey Mr. Justice,' and then he moved on to the next classroom," Newton recalled.

Now that he's unquestionably Charlotte's megastar athlete, he doesn't want that to be the case for the kids in this city. On Tuesday, he held his second annual Santa Cam Surprise Sleigh, making stops across the city and greeting children and fans for five hours.

Dressed in a red sweater with a black Santa Claus doing the dab, Newton began the afternoon at Metro School, which serves mentally and physically handicap children.

He, along with fellow Panthers quarterbacks Joe Webb and Derek Anderson, passed out cookies and other desserts to the children before Newton presented the 250-some teachers and staff there with $50 Belk gift cards.

Sy Bannister has been an assistant at the school for two years, and she's seen Newton at the school a handful of times. The children may not be able to express their excitement, but she sees the moods and attitudes change when the starting quarterback comes around.

"The kids love it all," Bannister said. "There's not a lot of verbal (communication) around here, but when he comes around, Cam is the man."

Perhaps the reaction in town would be the same for anyone playing quarterback at an MVP level on a 13-0 team. But there's something about Newton that connects with children.

There are the football giveaways, of course. And he has long said he wants to play the game with a child-like spirit.

The dabbin' and the dancing, the picture posing and the pumping up of the crowd all are part of Newton wanting to not only live in this moment, but have everyone along for the ride.

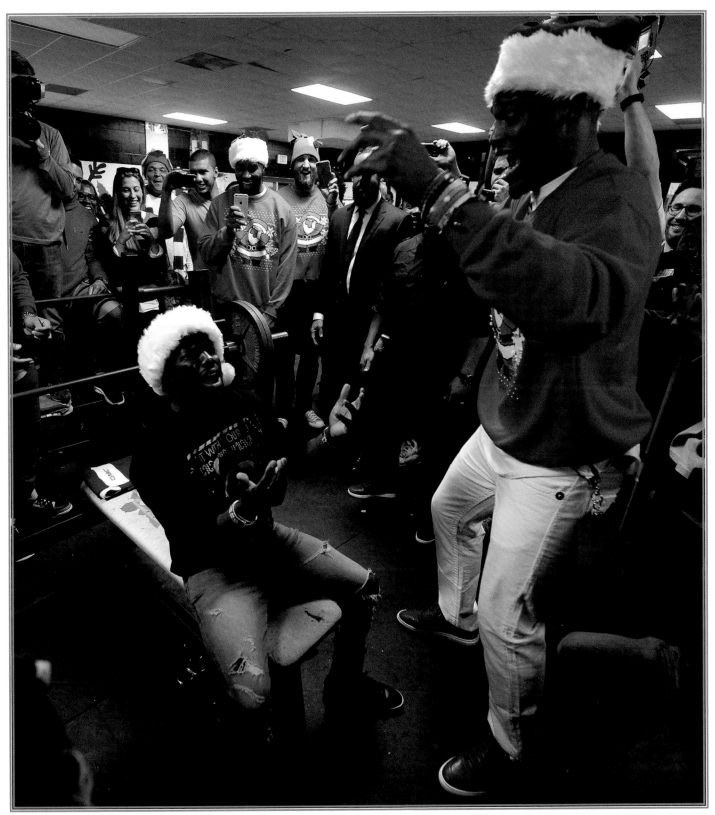

Cam Newton cheers as actor/comedian Kevin Hart prepares to bench press 225 pounds in Harding University High School's weight room December 15, 2015. Newton, Hart and actor/musician Ice Cube were there as part of Newton's Santa Cam Surprise Sleigh event, in which Newton traveled across the city, visiting kids and making donations. He presented Harding with $7,500 to refurbish the weight room (and Hart benched the weight three times). (Observer Photo/Jeff Siner)

"This doesn't happen often. It really doesn't," Newton said in the car between stops. "As long as we have the opportunity to set history, I would regret setting history and not being able to create lasting impressions or memories.

"I think I'm making it the time of my life because every day I get another opportunity."

ALL PART OF THE PLAN

The second stop on the tour brought Newton and his elves to Dick's Sporting Goods at SouthPark Mall. Twenty-five underserved elementary schoolers were gathered in the back of the store to hear a speech from a store manager when they were surprised by Newton, who gave each

Above: Cam Newton thanks Metro School students for their support during Newton's 2015 Santa Cam Surprise Sleigh event. Opposite: Newton uses a scooter to make his way around a Charlotte Dick's Sporting Goods store. Newton held a shopping spree for 25 children. (Observer Photos/Jeff Siner)

one a $200 gift card and helped them pick out Christmas gifts.

He gives them 10 minutes to shop and says if they don't get it done in that time, the cards will lose $195 of their value. When he notices his joke has produced some worried faces, he promises them an extra 10 minutes.

During a Q&A time, Isaiah — a fifth-grader with a bleached fohawk, a style made popular by Giants receiver Odell Beckham Jr. — had a question.

"What you got, little Odell?" Newton asked.

"Y'all not gonna lose, are you?" Isaiah asked.

"That's the plan," Newton said.

ACCESSIBLE TO FANS

There's nothing in Newton or any other player's contract that states they have to do these events. Few would expect the quarterback of an undefeated team to feed 900 kids on a short week before a Thanksgiving game against Dallas, or make a long night longer by hosting kids on the field after a 38-0 victory over Atlanta, or do all he did Tuesday, his day off.

But he got his treatment and film study in on Monday and was able to put aside enough time to focus on Tuesday's events when they came.

"It's one of the things we talked about in the offseason actually," Panthers offensive coordinator Mike Shula said. "Just to make

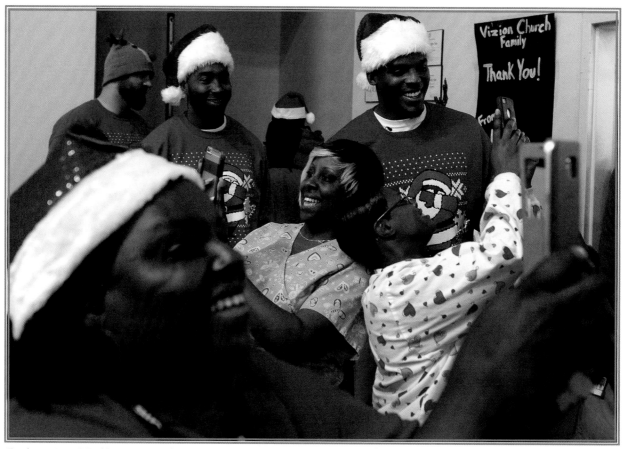

Faculty at Metro School hurry to take selfies with Panthers players Derek Anderson (left), Joe Webb (center) and Cam Newton. (Observer Photo/Jeff Siner)

sure that the season, we're locked in. If there's anything that goes on, it's got to be ... can't take any time or effort away from winning games each week, and he's very mindful of that."

Last week, on his way back from the stadium on the one-year anniversary of his car accident, Newton was stopped on the sidewalk by a young man who wanted to take a picture.

The kid told Newton he had actually received one of the Sunday Giveaway touchdown footballs. Newton couldn't believe it, and the kid pulled out his phone and showed Newton the picture of the moment at a Panthers home game.

"One thing I respected about Muhammad Ali — and I have the utmost respect for him — is any time you see documentaries about him or reading about him, he would always be accessible to his fans," Newton said. "He would just be so personable to his fans. And that's what I want people to say about me."

A WEIGHT IS LIFTED

Newton made it to Harding University High for his third stop, and this time he was joined by two of the most well-known names in show business. Rapper/actor Ice Cube and actor/comedian Kevin Hart were in town promoting their new movie, "Ride Along 2," and their schedules matched up.

Newton surprised student-athletes working out in the weight room by showing up with Under Armour gear. Then he introduced Ice Cube and Hart and the noise got even louder.

Ice Cube, a former gangster rapper whose image has softened since the early '90s, let Hart take center stage. The

students and Newton dared the 5-foot-4 Hart to bench press 225 pounds.

Hart took them up on it, benched the weight three times and then dabbed.

"Your dreams are only as small as your mindset allows you to be," Hart told the high schoolers. "You got a vision, you keep that vision. You stay true to your vision. You're looking at three men who were determined to get to where they got, man. You don't get there by being a person that quits and gives up. You don't do that.

"Understand this man is taking this out of his time. We're following his lead. It's his city. I love the fact that he's devoting his time to coming back and inspiring young people like yourself. Don't take that for granted."

FINALLY, A RIOT

The night ended around 6:30 p.m. at Dilworth Neighborhood Grille. Nearly 130 Panthers fans gathered downstairs for what they thought was a thank you from Zack Luttrell, the founder of Carolina's unofficial fan group, Roaring Riot.

In, of course, walks Newton. He says a few words and thanks everyone for their support. Most everyone in turn wants to see Newton or take a picture with him.

Newton spots Braylon Beam, the 6-year-old boy from Denver who has battled cancer and has been Carolina's honorary coach several times this year.

"What are you doing here?" Newton asked Beam after they did their usual chest bump. "I heard it's an 18-and-up-party!"

Like usual, Newton looked after the kids first. ✪

NBA superstar Stephen Curry hits the Keep Pounding drum at Levi's Stadium before Super Bowl 50. (Observer Photo/Jeff Siner)

Two of a Kind

Different in Style, Newton and Kuechly Are Surprisingly Similar

By Scott Fowler | February 4, 2016

At first glance, Cam Newton and Luke Kuechly seem to have little in common.

Newton is African-American, stylish and the life of every party he attends. Kuechly is white, admittedly un-stylish and content to stay on the sidelines everywhere except on the field.

"Cam walks into a room and lights it up," Carolina Panthers coach Ron Rivera said Wednesday. "Luke has this ability to kind of sneak in."

Newton said Wednesday that he and Kuechly were the "yin-yang twins."

But look closer. The two best and most important Carolina Panthers players in Sunday's Super Bowl 50 against Denver have far more similarities than you might imagine.

Among them: Relentless competitiveness. Great study habits. Superior talent. And a good sense of humor.

They tease each other constantly. Newton either calls Kuechly by his middle name ("August") or ribs him with the "Captain America" nickname he once bestowed upon him. Kuechly surprised everyone — especially Newton — when he dressed up as the quarterback for a team meeting in celebration of Halloween.

In a prank helped along by linebacker Thomas Davis, Kuechly raided Newton's locker for some way-too-big cleats and practice pants.

"Then all you've got to do is find some headphones and a Gatorade towel, throw that on, smile, put the kneepads on and all that stuff, and you're good to go," Kuechly said.

Rivera said it was "hysterical" to see the team's reaction, although Newton tried to play it cool at first. "I think when he first saw me, he was trying to act like it wasn't funny, but it was only a matter of time

Luke Kuechly (59) and Cam Newton (1) walk together between drills during Panthers training camp in August 2012. (Observer Photo/David T. Foster III)

before his big smile came out," Kuechly said.

'COMPETITIVE ENVIOUSNESS'

Newton joined the Panthers as the No. 1 overall pick in 2011. Kuechly came in 2012 at the No. 9 overall spot. Both were immediately successful, winning various rookie of the year honors. But Newton honed his work habits when he saw the way Kuechly prepared.

"He put so much pressure on me when he first got here, staying late, watching extra film, making sure that everyone on the defensive side knows what they're doing," Newton said of Kuechly. "For me watching, it was a competitive enviousness that I grew, and I was like, 'Dang, he gets it.'"

Newton started staying later at Bank of America Stadium more frequently, and it has become something of a competition now. Kuechly likes to peek into the quarterbacks' meeting room when he leaves at night, trying to see whether Newton is still in there studying opponents' film for the next game.

"I want to see who's going to be the last to leave," Kuechly said. "It goes back and forth."

Sometimes, Kuechly closes the building down — like when Rivera had to kick him out on Christmas Eve. Other times, Kuechly said, "Cam's in there with all the lights off and his headphones on, watching film."

Luke Kuechly greets a smiling Cam Newton after the Panthers' November 2012 win over Washington at FedEx Field. (Observer Photo/David T. Foster III)

Said Rivera: "They are opposites in some ways. But for the most part, I think they are a lot more similar than people realize ... Their commitment to whatever they do is tremendous."

NO FOXTAILS, NO VERSACE

The two have their differences, of course. Size is one.

Although you would think a linebacker would be bigger than a quarterback, it's not true in this case. Davis snapped a photo at Halloween of Kuechly in Newton garb and Newton smiling beside him and in on the joke, posting it on Instagram. Kuechly — generously listed at 6-foot-3, probably closer to 6-1 — is standing on his tiptoes to try and approach the height of the 6-5 Newton.

And there's the style question. Newton has his own clothing line, has posed for GQ and wore those pants (which retail for $849) on the team plane to the Super Bowl. Kuechly normally wears jeans and T-shirts and joked Wednesday that he needed to accept some fashion tips from Newton — within reason.

"There are certain things he can wear that I can't," Kuechly said. "I don't think I can pull off the foxtail. I don't think I'm cool enough to pull off the Versace pants. I'm going to start with baby steps."

There's also the likability factor. Kuechly is not as well-known nationally as Newton, but you'd be hard-pressed to ever find someone who says they can't stand him. Women hold up posters at stadiums asking to date him. Men wear his jerseys, too. Everyone yells "L-U-U-K-E" after he makes a big hit.

As for Newton, his popularity among kids and young adults is tremendous. And no Panthers player has ever come close to the quarterback in terms of endorsement value and national commercials. But he has his share of detractors — those who don't like the dancing, or the photo ops, or the Superman pose.

Newton described both sides of that fence Wednesday, saying there's a "Damn, Cam's cool" faction but also a "Hell, I hate Cam" faction.

CAN THE MAGIC CONTINUE?

In the playoffs, Newton and Kuechly have both been wondrous. Kuechly became the first player in NFL history to return an interception for a touchdown in consecutive games in a single postseason. And he has been a sure tackler as always.

"He gets there very quickly," Rivera, the former NFL linebacker, said of Kuechly. "And as the old saying goes, he arrives in a bad mood."

Newton is 26, and Kuechly is 24. They have both signed long-term deals with the Panthers, meaning the "yin-yang twins" will be this team's dual foundations for several years. ✪

Luke Kuechly and Cam Newton pose together in August 2013. By 2015, the duo emerged as the two most famous faces of the Panthers franchise. (Observer Photo/Jeff Siner)

Panthers players (from left) Thomas Davis, Ryan Kalil, Luke Kuechly, Greg Olsen, Cam Newton and Charles Johnson celebrate after beating Arizona for the NFC title.
(Observer Photo/Jeff Siner)

Newton Named MVP

Quarterback Receives 48 of 50 Votes, Becomes First Panther to Win Award

By Jonathan Jones | February 7, 2016

Cam Newton won the NFL's Most Valuable Player award Saturday night, and he'll be looking to add a Lombardi Trophy Sunday.

The fifth-year starting quarterback of the Carolina Panthers became the first player in team history to win the award. Ron Rivera, Newton's coach, won his second Coach of the Year award in three seasons.

"Without the fans there wouldn't be no me. Thank you for supporting me in an unwavering way for so much of my career," said Newton in a taped message at the NFL Honors ceremony since he couldn't be at the awards show the night before Super Bowl 50.

"I would also like to thank every person that has doubted me because you make me better."

Newton led the Panthers to a franchise-best 15-1 record and the No. 1 seed in the

NFC. He threw for 3,837 passing yards with a 59.7 completion percentage along with a career-high 35 passing touchdowns and career-low 10 interceptions.

Newton also had 10 rushing touchdowns to go along with his 636 rushing yards on 132 carries, the second-most by a quarterback in the Super Bowl era.

Newton won the award with 48 of the 50 possible votes. The Associated Press award is voted upon by journalists, analysts and former players at the end of the regular season. Arizona quarterback Carson Palmer and New England quarterback Tom Brady each got one vote.

Newton's quarterback counterpart in Super Bowl 50, Peyton Manning, said this week that Newton had an "incredible year."

"I mean, no doubt in my mind he's going to be the MVP on Saturday night," said Manning, who has won the award an

Cam Newton wore gold MVP shoes during pregame for Super Bowl 50, before swapping them out for regular shoes for the actual game. (Observer Photo/Jeff Siner)

Cam Newton and the Panthers celebrate following Carolina's 49-15 victory over the Arizona Cardinals in the NFC Championship Game. (Observer Photo/Jeff Siner)

NFL-record five times. "What he's done in the short time being an NFL quarterback he's been awesome. It's the best word I can think of.

"He's been a great passer, he's been a great runner, he's been a great leader. You don't go 17-1 as a starting quarterback without being awesome and that's what he's been this year without a doubt."

Newton is also the first African-American quarterback to win the award outright. Steve McNair shared the award with Manning in 2003.

Newton, who also won the AP Offensive Player of the Year award with 18 votes, becomes the first Panthers player in team history to even receive an MVP vote.

"The last time I spoke on Cam's behalf it didn't go very well so I'm going to be very brief," Newton's dad, Cecil, said when accepting the Offensive Player of the Year award when making an apparent reference to the pay-for-play scheme during Newton's collegiate years.

Rivera won the highest honor for coaches for the second time since 2013. He received the award after Carolina's 12-4 season.

Rivera ran away with the award's voting, earning 36½ of the 50 votes. Kansas City coach Andy Reid was second with six votes.

"An award like this is indicative of the organization and ours start at the top with our owner, Mr. (Jerry) Richardson, and also with our general manager, Dave Gettleman, who's been very supportive in the last few years and been behind me the whole way," Rivera said.

Panthers offensive coordinator Mike Shula finished third in voting for the AP's assistant coach of the year award. Shula oversaw the league's No. 1 scoring offense in 2015.

Denver defensive coordinator Wade Phillips won the award with 18 votes. Former Cincinnati offensive coordinator

Hue Jackson had nine votes, and Shula finished with seven votes.

Middle linebacker Luke Kuechly finished in third place for the AP Defensive Player of the Year award that he won in 2013. Kuechly had four votes while cornerback Josh Norman finished in fourth with two votes.

Houston Texans defensive end J.J. Watt won the award for the third time in his career with 37 votes. ✪

Fans enter Levi's Stadium for Super Bowl 50. (Observer Photo/Todd Sumlin)

CAM MOMENT

THE SUPER BOWL FASHION STATEMENT

Cam Newton began the Carolina Panthers' journey to the Super Bowl in characteristic style: Surprising, joyful and a little in-your-face: Zebra patterned pants with looping gold swirls that fashion aficionados could guess.

We believe them to be Versace — "Barocco Accent Print Jeans" in Yellow Zebraprint, to be specific — from our perusal of lyst.com, a shopping aggregation site (for $849).

Now, on to those shoes...

—Helen Schwab

Super Bowl Letdown

Cam Didn't Succeed as a Role Model

By Jonathan Jones | February 9, 2016

How would you have handled sitting in front of dozens of reporters answering questions 30 minutes later?

Maybe you would have handled it better than Cam — not sighing and giving mostly one-word responses before walking out abruptly three minutes later.

But here's the problem with that. We are not like Cam. He is not like us.

Newton is held to a standard to which we — media, fans, observers — hold most superstar athletes. Win or lose a big game, you have to face the music. That's the deal he struck when he signed up for professional football, and that's especially the deal when he, for the better part of five years, has said around the world that he wants to be a role model for children.

First, let's take the Super Bowl 50 postgame news conference for what it is. Newton, scowling in the locker room after the toughest defeat of his career, had to go to a podium in front of hungry media on deadline and answer some decent, some inane questions about the events of the night.

I was still in Carolina's locker room and wasn't present for Newton's questioning. But I know the setup in that auxiliary news conference area, and I've watched the video several times.

Though he gave mostly monosyllabic answers, he was capable of answering questions. We know that because he answered one, and it was in response to a question that he shut down with a "no" earlier in the session.

"They just played better than us," said Newton, who was named the league MVP the night before. "I don't know what you want me to say, I'm sorry. They made more plays than us, and that's what it came down to. We had opportunities. It wasn't nothing special that they did. We dropped balls, we turned the ball over, gave up sacks, threw errant passes. That's it, they scored more points than us."

The pain of the Super Bowl loss was evident on Cam Newton's face as he walked the sideline as the Broncos ran down the clock late in the game. (Observer Photo/David T. Foster III)

Nearby, victorious cornerback Chris Harris Jr. could be heard eagerly responding to a question about how the Denver defense shut down Carolina's passing game.

Newton — deciding that whatever this was, wasn't worth it — said he was done and left the podium with a team spokesman.

That the losing quarterback, or any member of the losing team, has to essentially share the stage with the winners is an unfair request by the NFL.

Levi's Stadium was made, in part, to host big events such as the Super Bowl. The respective team's mascots had their own room on the ground floor of the cavernous building.

They should have found somewhere else to stick the Panthers rather than have to hear the Broncos in ecstasy.

While that is going on, we media members expect these athletes on the losing squad to bare their souls. "How does this feel?" we ask, as if we don't already know that summoning any kind of words

Cam Newton reaches for the ball after losing a fumble during Super Bowl 50. (Observer Photo/David T. Foster III)

for an indescribable feeling is impossible enough.

We, the sports-writing media, think too highly of ourselves. We remain the conduit for fans, but that rope frays with every new social media app made available or publicist hired. Only country music singers give themselves more awards than sports writers.

For the past two years, Seattle running back Marshawn Lynch gave the media nothing during Super Bowl week. It turned into "the" story of the week, with writers taking torches to Lynch for not carrying out his obligation.

"I'm just here so I won't get fined," he famously said.

But that's Lynch, and that's his brand. He's the guy who retired during the Super Bowl on Sunday night and made the announcement by taking a picture of cleats tied together and thrown on a powerline. Why should you, or we, expect more?

Newton has carried out his media obligations all week, even if there was some eye-rolling and sighing during some lagging portions of it. He was getting the same questions over and over again, and he let it be known by Thursday.

"It means a lot," said Newton when asked about his close relationship with tight end Greg Olsen.

"I'm sorry if I'm bland," Newton said Thursday when asked about wearing the hospital bracelet from his December 2014 car accident, "but, man, I've been asked that question thousands of times. To be respectful, it means a lot. Obviously, it's a life-changing moment in my life."

There is precedent for sports figures not playing nice with media and people loving it. San Antonio Spurs coach Gregg Poppovich is famous for his five NBA titles and his mastery of avoiding any question during an in-game interview.

Sometimes Patriots coach Bill Belichick seemingly doesn't bother waking up to answer questions (unless you ask him about left-footed punters or the best blocking tight ends in NFL history, and then he'll fill up your notebook).

I have interviewed both, and I believe I have asked good questions to both. And I didn't get much of a quote from either one of them.

It's not endearing to me, but that's who they are. They make no bones about it.

Newton, meanwhile, will play the game. He's been especially good at his news conferences since the Thanksgiving Day win against Dallas, when the spotlight began to shine brighter on him and his team.

Even in Atlanta, after losing Carolina's only game of the regular season just days after the birth of his first son, Newton sulked at his locker for at least 30 minutes and then sucked it up and stood at the podium and took several questions.

My colleague Scott Fowler asked Hall of Fame cornerback Deion Sanders, who expressed his confidence arguably more than any other player in his generation, what he thought of the way the Panthers play the game, and Deion was prophetic.

"Let me tell you the difference," Sanders said. "I play like that when I lose. There's a difference. It's easy to have joy when you're winning. But you've got to keep that joy when you're getting your butt kicked too. You've got to keep that same swagger, that same confidence. That's real. When you 17-1, oh it's easy. Yeah."

It's one thing to give fuel to Sanders, an NFL Network analyst who regularly and shamelessly makes outlandish characterizations and inserts himself into stories.

But it's another to give fuel to all the haters that Newton mentioned in his taped MVP speech.

Those same people — from those of an older generation, to opposing teams' fans and to those scrambling for ways to explain their distaste for Newton without using coded racist language — were served a perfect example. This is the ammunition

Cam Newton walks off the field after the Panthers' 24-10 loss to the Denver Broncos in Super Bowl 50. (Observer Photo/David T. Foster III)

they can use for the cold months of Newton's offseason.

But this is about more than these haters who don't have Band-Aids for their feelings, as Newton said in his latest Beats by Dre national commercial. This is about a person who wants to be great on the field and a cultural force off it.

Newton has built up a great deal of capital with his play on the field and

his actions off it. He's acknowledged his college-age mistakes, and we should have moved past them by now. And he has reached thousands of children.

For that and his play on the field, Newton became a role model — willingly.

Too often we look to athletes as role models when we shouldn't, or when they don't want us to. Former NBA star Charles Barkley famously told us all that he is not a role model, and with that admission he has carved out quite the career as the say-anything TV analyst, even though his basketball exploits fade away with each crop of new NBA stars.

But Newton is a role model, and he embraces it. This is what he has set out to do from day one.

"I'm given a stage, and what I do on that stage means a lot," Newton said Wednesday, "because for people who I'm going to actually meet and for people that's watching this live and saying, 'Damn, Cam's cool.' For these same people that are saying, 'Hell, I hate Cam,' either way, I'm going to stay true to who I am and try to fulfill the things that are important to me.

"For anybody that's (following in my footsteps), I want to make the road as clear as possible, because those are the same things that help me."

There were factors at play Sunday night that caused Newton to react how he did after the loss, and hopefully the NFL works out its kinks in Super Bowls to come.

There is no contract for being a role model, but there is a deal in place. Millions were watching after Super Bowl 50, and Newton didn't hold up his end. ✪

Cam Newton speaks with reporters in Charlotte two days after Super Bowl 50. (Observer Photo/T. Ortega Gaines)

Cam Responds to Critics

'Who Likes to Lose?' Not Newton

By Jonathan Jones | February 10, 2016

Two days after the biggest football loss of his life, Carolina Panthers quarterback Cam Newton still had no regrets about his handling of the post-game news conference.

After the 24-10 loss in Super Bowl 50, a downtrodden Newton appeared for less than 3 minutes in front of media, answered just one question with more than a few words and eventually got up and left the podium.

"We've got all these people who are condemning and saying, 'Oh he should have done this, that and the third,' but what makes your way right?" Newton said Tuesday at his locker in Bank of America Stadium.

"I've been on record to say I'm a sore loser. Who likes to lose? You show me a good loser and I'm going to show you a loser."

In his previous four seasons in the league, Newton has never talked to media during exit interviews. Tuesday he clearly had topics he wanted to address, and he answered questions for more than 7 minutes on the much-talked-about topics of his news conference and his failure to dive on a fumble late in the game.

"Well I ain't got no more tears to cry," Newton opened on his reflections from the Super Bowl. "I've had a lot of time to think about. I've seen so much blown out of proportion. At the end of the day when you invest so much time, when you sacrifice so much and things don't go as planned, I think emotions take over. I think that's what happens."

Newton offered few words Sunday night after the loss. He appeared at a podium in the bowels of Levi's Stadium in his game-worn pants and a black hoodie.

Newton, usually dapper in his post-game news conferences, put on the hoodie to expedite a process of getting ready that is among the longest in the league for star players.

With Denver cornerback Chris Harris Jr. excitedly answering questions about how the Broncos shut down Newton and

Carolina's passing game, Newton got up from the podium saying "I'm done" and went back to the locker room.

NOT 'OTHER PLAYERS'

Panthers coach Ron Rivera didn't necessarily defend all of Newton's post-game actions, but he did posit that players who especially don't take well to losing should be given more time.

"What we're asking people to do in a stressful situation after a very difficult situation is to gather our composure and step up right away," Rivera said. "I'm not sure how fair that is. I'm really not. And he's not the only player that's ever been through a situation like that and handled it like that."

Other players have handled it better. Seattle quarterback Russell Wilson threw one of the biggest interceptions in Super Bowl history last week and faced the music. Denver's Peyton Manning lost by 35 the year before and took his medicine, too.

Newton had heard those comparisons several times in the past two days and didn't care for them.

"I've heard numerous quotes about, 'What if this person was in this situation? How would he have handled it? Well we've seen this person do that, how would he have handled it?' The truth of the matter is I'm not trying to be that person, nor am I trying to be that person," Newton said. "I've said it since Day One. I am who I am. I know what I'm capable of, and I know where I'm going. I don't have to conform to anybody else's wants for me to do. I'm not that guy.

"If you want me to be this type of person, I'm not that. And I'm happy to say that. This league is a great league with or without me. And I am my own person. I take pride in that and that's pretty much how I feel."

RIVERA ADDRESSES 'SORE LOSER' BALANCE

Asked if he and the team embrace Newton's sore loser mentality, Rivera found a balance.

"Well I wouldn't say we like it," Rivera said. "We don't want to promote it, most certainly there are a lot of young people that are out there looking at who we are. And we are role models for them.

"And I think again, I don't want to say we accept it but we know who he is. He does take it hard. And quite honestly if he's going to take it hard, then maybe, maybe, as a public service we can avoid having him talk right away."

Ultimately, Rivera admitted he would have liked his quarterback to handle the situation better and differently.

But the coach also knows that's who Newton is. He wears his emotion on his sleeve. It's great when they're winning and it's bad when they're losing.

If this was supposed to be a learning experience, though, Newton didn't seem to absorb it. He said he had no regrets while standing at his locker.

"For me," Newton said, "nothing's pretty much going to change. You get what you get." ✪

Cam Newton reacts after a pass interference penalty was called on the Panthers' defense during the fourth quarter of Super Bowl 50. (Observer Photo/David T. Foster III)

10 Moments that Shaped Cam Newton's Career

By Joseph Person

I've covered virtually every step of Cam Newton's career — including some of his dance steps — since the Panthers quarterback arrived in Charlotte as the city's biggest sports star in the spring of 2011.

I've been there for the highs, the lows and a couple of scares, including the December day in 2014 when Newton rolled his truck outside the *Observer*'s former offices.

A look at 10 moments that shaped Newton's first five NFL seasons.

SEPTEMBER 11, 2011

NFL owners had locked out players during a labor dispute after the Panthers drafted Newton No. 1 overall. Without offseason practices and minicamp canceled, there was a lot of discussion about whether Newton's timing with his receivers would be off early in his rookie season.

Not so much.

Newton sparkled in his debut at Arizona, passing for 422 yards and two touchdowns in the same stadium where he led Auburn to college football's national championship eight months earlier. Though it was in a losing effort, Newton became the first rookie to throw for more than 400 yards in his first game.

DECEMBER 18, 2011

It wasn't so much about how Newton played in a 28-13 victory at Houston, but how he comported himself. Newton had come under fire for hanging his towel-covered head on the sideline and sulking in post-game press conferences as the losses mounted during his rookie year.

Veteran offensive linemen Jordan Gross and Ryan Kalil talked to Newton about his demeanor before the Titans' game, and Newton responded by keeping his negative emotions in check.

After the Texans rallied in the second half, Newton encouraged his offensive teammates in the huddle before the Panthers went on a long touchdown drive to seal the victory.

Cam Newton celebrates after scoring a touchdown during the Panthers' home victory over the Green Bay Packers on November 8, 2015. (Observer Photo/Jeff Siner)

JANUARY 8, 2013

Panthers coach Ron Rivera's future had been in doubt before he received a vote of confidence from owner Jerry Richardson after two losing seasons. Now Rivera had to hire an offensive coordinator to replace Rob Chudzinski, who left to become Cleveland's head coach.

Rivera interviewed former Browns coach Pat Shurmur and Hue Jackson (currently Cleveland's coach) before promoting Mike Shula from quarterbacks coach. Rivera wanted to keep things stable for Newton, who had played for three schools before being drafted.

Panthers offensive coordinator Mike Shula talks with Cam Newton in 2013. (Observer Photo/Jeff Siner)

Shula tweaked a couple of things, but an offensive system that took advantage of Newton's running and passing skills stayed largely the same.

NOVEMBER 18, 2013

Newton had only engineered two game-winning drives his first two seasons, and the doubters wondered about his ability to perform in the clutch. A week before the first-place Panthers' Monday Night Football clash with New England, Newton led Carolina to a comeback victory at San Francisco.

That set up the highly anticipated home game with the Patriots, who led 20-17 with 6:32 remaining. Taking over at the Carolina 17, Newton accounted for 72 yards (57 passing, 15 rushing) and gave the Panthers the lead on a 25-yard touchdown pass to Ted Ginn Jr. in the final minute.

When the Panthers survived a Tom Brady throw to Rob Gronkowski in the end zone (and a waved-off pass interference penalty on Luke Kuechly), Newton had his first big, signature victory.

DECEMBER 9, 2014

Around lunchtime on the players' day off, Newton was driving his 1998 Dodge pick-up when he collided with another vehicle on Church Street in the shadow of Bank of America Stadium.

Newton's truck rolled several times before coming to a stop on a bridge over I-277. Newton was hospitalized for a night with a lower back injury, and was back at the stadium two days later to receive treatment and attend meetings.

Panthers players pose before the end of Carolina's win over the Arizona Cardinals in the NFC Championship Game. (Observer Photo/ David T. Foster III)

Newton said the accident had given him a better sense of perspective.

"I'm on somebody's fantasy league, and I think it's the man upstairs," Newton said.

The Panthers didn't lose a regular-season game for more than a year after Newton's wreck.

JUNE 2, 2015

Under the new labor deal struck before his first season, Newton did not get the huge rookie contract quarterbacks such as JaMarcus Russell and Sam Bradford had received. Newton's first contract was worth $22 million guaranteed over four years.

But Newton struck it big in the summer of 2015 when the Panthers gave him a five-year, $103.8 million extension, including $60 million guaranteed.

In addition to the financial security, the new contract seemed to embolden Newton, who arrived at training camp last summer saying he wasn't like any other quarterback and as such didn't want to be judged that way.

The Panthers' investment paid off immediately, with a Super Bowl trip and a league MVP award for their newly minted quarterback.

SEPTEMBER 20, 2015

There are some things that 6-5, 260-pound quarterbacks aren't supposed to do, like flip over defenders into the end zone. But Newton often defies the normal characterizations of a quarterback — and the laws of gravity — leaving fans to marvel at his unique skill set.

Newton's 2-yard touchdown leap in a 24-17 victory over Houston in Week 2 was aired repeatedly in the days following and prompted some browbeating from some (see Esiason, Boomer) who thought it was extraneous and not worth the risk of injury.

"I'm in a lose-lose situation," Newton said. "If I would've run him over and something would've happened then, (people would have said), 'He's got to be more conscientious of how he runs. Cam's running too much.'"

OCTOBER 18, 2015

The Panthers were 4-0 when they headed west to Seattle but many observers weren't sold on them, saying they'd beaten up on sub-par teams. The Seahawks were in a different class, and Newton had gone winless (including playoffs) in four head-to-head matchups with Russell Wilson.

Carolina looked to be headed toward another close loss to Seattle before Newton marched the offense 80 yards in less than two minutes for a 27-23 victory.

Opposite: Cam Newton celebrates following the Panthers' NFC Championship Game victory over the Arizona Cardinals. (Observer Photo/Jeff Siner)

Above: Cam Newton reacts after throwing a game-winning touchdown pass to Greg Olsen to upset the Seahawks in Seattle in October 2015. (Observer Photo/David T. Foster III)

Newton was 6-of-7 passing (the only incompletion was a spike) for 89 yards on the game-winning drive, which he capped with a 26-yard touchdown pass to tight end Greg Olsen.

The Panthers would finish the regular season 15-1 and beat the Seahawks again in the playoffs en route to the second Super Bowl in franchise history.

JANUARY 24, 2016

The Panthers and Cardinals were the NFC's two best teams throughout the regular season, so it was only fitting they would meet in the NFC Championship Game in Charlotte with a berth in Super Bowl 50 at stake.

But it was never close — thanks in large part to Newton, who passed for 335 yards and accounted for four touchdowns to punch the Panthers' ticket to Santa Clara. The Panthers won 49-15, racking up the highest point total in NFC Championship Game history.

"We did what a lot of people said we couldn't do. It's not over, yet," Newton said from the makeshift stage over chants of "MVP!"

Cam Newton leaps into the end zone to score during the third quarter of the NFC Championship Game on January 24. 2016. (Observer Photo/Jeff Siner)

Members of the Carolina Panthers including Luke Kuechly, Charles Johnson, Greg Olsen, Thomas Davis and Cam Newton hold up the George Halas Trophy after winning the NFC Championship over the Arizona Cardinals. (Observer Photo/David T. Foster III)

FEBRUARY 6, 2016

Newton's place among the league's best players was cemented the night before the Super Bowl when he received 48 of 50 votes for MVP. A videotaped message from Newton was played at the NFL Honors ceremony while Newton was at the team's San Jose hotel.

Newton became the sixth Heisman Trophy winner to win the MVP, and had hoped to join Marcus Allen as the only players to win a Heisman, national title in college, MVP and a Super Bowl.

It was not to be as the Panthers fell to Denver 24-10 the following night. But with Newton, 27, just hitting his prime, there's every reason to believe he'll be in the MVP conversation most seasons and have the Panthers in contention for a Super Bowl ring. ✪

Cam Newton dances in the end zone after scoring a touchdown against the Dallas Cowboys on November 26, 2015. The Panthers won 33-14 to improve to 11-0 on the season. (Observer Photo/David T. Foster III)